HOW THEY TRAIN
Second Edition
Fred Wilt, editor

VOLUME III:
SPRINTING AND HURDLING

Publishing history, How They Train:
    First printing, June 1959
    Second printing, January 1960
    Third printing, August 1962
    Fourth printing, December 1965
    Fifth printing, September 1968
    Sixth printing, March 1970

    Second edition, completely revised, in
    three volumes:

    Vol. I: Middle Distances, March 1973
    Vol. II: Long Distances, June 1973
    Vol. III: Sprinting And Hurdling, June 1973

Other books by Fred Wilt:
    Run Run Run, 1964
    Illustrated Guide to Olympic Track & Field
        Techniques (with Tom Ecker), 1969
    Mechanics Without Tears, 1970
    International Track & Field Coaching
        Encyclopedia (with Tom Ecker), 1970
    Motivation and Coaching Psychology (with
        Ken Bosen), 1971
    The Jumps: Contemporary Theory, Technique
        and Training, 1972

Library of Congress No.: 73-76249
Standard Book No.: 0-911520-47-3

Printed in the United States of America

INTRODUCTION TO THE FIRST EDITION

As a 14-year old freshman in a small Indiana high school, I was the only miler on the track team. Track training knowledge was unknown to my coach and others in the area. To better prepare myself for maximum performances, two or three times a week I would train by running a slow two-mile. This was due to the erroneous personal assumption that if I could endure two miles in training, one mile in a race should be easy. But each race was a bitter experience in terms of exhaustion, and I suffered many infuriating defeats at the hands of athletes from larger schools who had the benefit of better coaching and more thorough workout programs. I consulted what literature I could find on the subject of training, but found nothing specific which I could actually use.

In 1940, I enrolled at Indiana University and came under the influence of America's most successful middle distance coach, the late E.C. (Billy) Hayes. Within two months my mile improved from 4:35 to 4:22 and my two-mile from 10:10 to 9:22. Racing which had before meant only pain and exhaustion, now provided me with a feeling of joy in conquering personal fatigue. Hayes taught me the what, how, and why of training as he knew it. By following his advice I was able to achieve results previously unimaginable to me.

The coaching success of Billy Hayes was no mere accident. He had a system of training which recognized the individual differences among runners and took into consideration the physiological factors in running. Yet his system was developed primarily through trial and error. He was an Olympic coach in 1936, once toured Scandinavia with an American team, constantly searched for better methods, paid particular attention to the training of others, continually re-examined his own system, and was always willing to change his methods in favor of something better.

Billy Hayes passed away in 1943. Since then, many changes have taken place in training methods generally accepted throughout the world. While the basic principles of training may remain the same, the application of these principles is better understood and applied more universally. This is evidenced by faster performances. Thus in writing this book I have attempted to illustrate the evolution of training methods by describing the actual workout programs of great athletes from 1900 to the present time. Actually, in preparing this book for publication, I have been more of a compiler than a writer, and whenever possible I have let the athletes use their own words in describing their training programs.

The world's first sub-four minute miler, Dr. Roger G. Bannister, has said that "training methods . . . being dependent upon more factors than it is possible at present to analyze, are likely to remain empirical." I wholeheartedly concur, but hasten to add that no empirical training procedure should ever violate known scientific or physiological facts. After a training procedure has been developed through trial and error, it should be possible to justify it on a physiological basis—otherwise it must be subject to question.

You often see items in the press purporting to fabulous workouts by athletes. Much was made of Zatopek having run sixty 440's in a single workout. Yet had he run these 440's in only 85 or 90 seconds it would not have been too much of an accomplishment. It means very little to say the training of an athlete on a specific day involves 10x440 yards. On the other hand, it means very much to say that this workout involved one mile warm-up jogging in eight minutes, followed by 10x440 yards in 62 seconds each, jogging 440 yards in 2½ minutes between each fast quarter, and finally one mile warm-down jogging in 10 minutes. That is why I have attempted to be quite specific in obtaining information on the training of each athlete. To warn youngsters of the grave danger in using the same training as a mature athlete such as Vladimir Kuts or Derek Ibbotson would be rather begging the obvious. This is elementary, and probably something a youngster could not accomplish. I do not recommend that any athlete copy the training procedure of another, but I do maintain that the material herein will suggest many ideas which may be adopted in formulating workout programs suited to an individual runner's needs. Just as no two athletes have identical form, so no two athletes need have the same training program. Literally, as well as figuratively, there is more than one road to Rome. A youngster should not let the herculean training program of top athletes, as described in this book, discourage him. By using a training program involving gradual adaption to stress over a prolonged period of time, workouts consisting of both quality and quantity may be accomplished. However, intensive training absolutely does not insure successful racing. The training merely makes successful racing possible. A runner must also have the all-important factor of mental attitude, a will to win, a subconscious desire for victory, courage, tenacity, and a competitive "killer instinct" in order to achieve racing success.

My own twenty years of competitive racing have been a beneficial experience in many ways. Through the sport of track I have enjoyed many pleasant associations which probably would not have been otherwise available to me. It is probably thus fitting that I should attempt to make some tangible contribution to the sport in token of appreciation. My attempted contribution is an effort to disseminate empirical (not scientific) training knowledge.

I would like to thank the athletes and contributors who have made the presentation of this material possible. Special thanks go to Hal Higdon for the illustrations; to Bert and Cordner Nelson of "Track & Field News" for their obvious labor of love in publishing this; and to my beloved wife, Eleanor Hebsgaard Christensen, for doing so much (more than I like to admit) of the work involved.

Fred Wilt   July, 1959

PREFACE TO THIS EDITION

The first edition of HOW THEY TRAIN, originally printed in 1959, listed more than 150 runners and their training patterns, half mile to six miles and up. The popularity and value of this book was such that we thought a new edition, with some of the current top athletes, was clearly called for. We have been collecting material and sending out questionnaires for a number of years now. In fact, so much valuable material was obtained that it was decided to split HOW THEY TRAIN—II into three volumes. Thus, three separate books are now available: HOW THEY TRAIN—MIDDLE DISTANCES, HOW THEY TRAIN—LONG DISTANCES, and HOW THEY TRAIN—SPRINTING AND HURDLING. The last volume covers an area not previously handled and fills a need in the track community, we believe.

We are also reprinting some useful material from the first edition. The original introduction (above) is included as it indicates how a book on training programs should be approached by a beginning or veteran runner. Further, so that the very interesting (and still useful) training routines of some of the great athletes of the past would not pass into oblivion when the first edition of HTT went out of print, some of these entries are being reprinted. Thus, the training of Herb Elliott, John Landy, Emil Zatopek, Kuts, Hägg, Nurmi, Harbig, and others is reproduced in the appropriate books of the second edition, and provides very interesting comparisons with the training of today's champions.

Data on present-day athletes were obtained over a period of time, thus only a few will offer 1971 or 1972 training schedules. Steve Prefontaine and Dave Wottle, for instance, contributed their information in 1969, and their training then may have little relation to their build-ups for the 1972 Olympic Games. But both were good runners in 1969, and certainly their training for that year contains lessons and much of interest to any coach and runner.

Each entry lists the name of the athlete, his club or school, and his age and year when the training details were obtained. Also given in most cases are personal statistics (birth date, height and weight, when the athlete began running, etc.). And most entries divide the training year by seasons and end by giving details of strategy, personal philosophy, career history, etc., updated where necessary.

Not every runner in these pages is of world class caliber, but all are fairly well known, at least in the USA. This gives a mix of training programs of top-flight runners and lesser lights, which should be of value. This volume on sprinting and hurdling offers athletes with various specialties, 100-440 yards and 120-yard high hurdles to the 440-yard intermediates.

We'd once again like to express our sincere thanks to the athletes who shared their training ideas and procedures with us, and to the authors and publications who assisted in making available material included in this edition. Also, thanks to the following individuals for their kind efforts in assisting with the writing of profiles contained herein: Gary Childs, Bill Blewett, John T. Goegel, Alexander W. Saltmarsh, Don Kopriva, Joey Haines, Robert Hoffenberg, Larry J. Myers, Robert Henson, Ken Stone, Bill Huyck, Mark Green, John Boyd Scott, Larry Main, H. David Dunsky, Stuart Warner and Dr. Gordon N. Schafer.

ILLUSTRATIONS/PHOTO CREDITS

Page	Photo	Photographer
Cover	Valeriy Borzov	Tony Duffy
9	Valeriy Borzov	Jeff Kroot
12	Robbie Brightwell	Ed Lacey
14	Frank Budd	
17	Otis Davis	
21	Ed Lacey	
23	Mike Larrabee	Chuck James
24	Mike Larrabee	Ed Lacey
28	Adrian Metcalfe, Robbie Brightwell	Ed Lacey
28	Curtis Mills	Walley Brown
32	Bobby Morrow	
33	Wendell Mottley	Mark Shearman
34	Ira Murchison	Ed Lacey
38	Ray Norton	San Jose Mercury
38	Ray Norton	
40	Mel Patton	
45	Dave Sime	Ed Lacey
47	John Smith	Don Chadez
49	Ulis Williams	Ed Ryan
51	Lee Calhoun	
54	Rex Cawley	Eli Attar
57	Glenn Davis	Ken Dare, Los Angeles Times
58	Jack Davis	
58	Jack Davis	
62	Dave Hemery	Albert Session
65	Gary Knoke	Steve Murdock
68	Ralph Mann	Steve Murdock
75	Eddie Southern	"Duke" D'Ambra
76	Spencer Thomas	Knoxville News-Sentinel
79	Marcus Walker	Jim Ryun, Topeka Capital-Journal
80	Ron Whitney	Don Wilkinson

CONTENTS

Sprinting

Valeriy Borzov

Valeriy Borzov

VALERIY BORZOV, Physical Sports Institute of Kiev, Russia (USSR). Age 21 years, 1970.

BEST MARKS: 200m., 20.2 (European record); 100m., 10.0 (equal European record).

PERSONAL STATISTICS: Born October 20, 1949 at Lvov, Ukraine, USSR. 5'11½", 174 lbs.

TRAINING: Borzov came out of his home town's Youth Sports School at age 17 with best marks of 10.5m. and 22.0m. He joined coach Valentin Petrovski's training squad and became a guinea pig of sorts as he came under an entirely new and unique form of sprint training. After perfecting his sprint technique through uphill runs and intensive coaching, Borzov began a schedule of training based on his specific need for either speed or endurance. Coach Petrovski's studies with the use of an electro-myograph led him to believe that there was a close correlation between times taken over 30 and 60 meters with expected performances over the standard 100 and 200 meter distances respectively. "The correlations were set into tables and served as a guide to what Borzov had to achieve over 30 meter tests from month to month. In the early stages of Borzov's training with Petrovski it became obvious that, according to the tables, Borzov lacked speed. He was immediately set to work, according to Petrovski's speed training method, using fast sprints with long recoveries. They were mainly repetitions of 60m. from flying and crouch starts with emphasis on complete rest between the large number of repetitions. At the same time speed endurance was not overlooked and Borzov's training sessions included repetitive sprinting with limited recoveries. His tempo (interval) runs were mainly over 150 and 200 meters. . ., in addition to 30 minutes cross-country and occasional 800m. runs. In the development of speed Borzov covered between 2400-3200 meters in a training session. He stuck rigidly to the principle of full recoveries by increasing recovery times during a workout to assure near complete rest before the next repetition was started. Borzov's weekly training plan was based on constant changes in speed and speed endurance work. Usually Mondays served for medium speed repetitions, Tuesdays for speed development, etc. However, the program was flexible and alterations were made according to Petrovski's analysis of the day's workouts. The basis of the changes were the 30 and 60 meter tables. A drop in the 60m. performance was regarded as an indication of lack of speed endurance and the need for more work to develop it. Slower 30m. times suggested concentration on speed work."

SUMMER TRAINING: The outstanding feature of Borzov's summer training was an intensive development of speed. His running technique was now good and allowed him to concentrate on speed work. Speed endurance training, as described above, still remained in the program but was strictly carried out on separate days from speed training.

Valeriy Borzov adopted a "Lydiard" type philosophy holding that only a small amount of competitions should be considered important enough to train specifically for. In other words, he did not try to peak early in the season and keep his performances along an even plane, but train "through" the meets of lesser import and concentrate on races of value. The success of this philosophy was born out in 1970 and 1971 when he captured European and Russian sprint titles. *Track & Field News* also named him the No. 2 sprinter of 1970 for the 100m. dash. In 1971, he was No. 1 in the 100, second in the 200.

Valeriy Borzov had a banner year in 1972. He ran two 10.0 100s and took both sprints in the Olympic Games with 10.14 and 20.00 clockings, the latter a new European record, solidifying his claim as one of history's great sprinters.

Robbie Brightwell

ROBBIE IAN BRIGHTWELL, Loughborough Colleges A.C. and Birchfield Harriers. Age 23, 1962.

BEST MARKS: 400m., 44.9 (r); 220y, 21.3; 100y, 9.7.

PERSONAL STATISTICS: Born October 27, 1939 in Rawalpindi, Pakistan. 6'2", 168 lbs. Started racing at age 16.

PRE-RACE WARM-UP: Three laps easy jogging, 15 minutes stretching exercises. 4x100y, the last two being full speed. 3-4xstarts. Rest 10 minutes. Whole warm-up takes 45 minutes.

WINTER TRAINING: Monday: Rest. Tuesday: 10x150y repetitions in 16.5 with 3 minutes recovery. Wednesday: 4x300y repetitions in 34 with 5 minutes recovery. Thursday: 12 fast starts from blocks. Easy walk back. Friday: Weight training. Saturday: Cross-country or fartlek. Sunday: 10x220y intervals in 25-26 with 3 minutes recovery.

SPRING/SUMMER TRAINING: Monday: 6x150y repetitions in 14.5 with 3 minutes recovery. Tuesday: 12x100y repetitions in 10.0 with 2 minutes recovery. Wednesday: 3x220y in 22 with 5 minutes recovery. Thursday: 15xstarts from normal 440y starting position around the first turn. Recovery: walk slowly back to blocks. Friday: Rest. Saturday: Competition. Sunday: Easy fartlek on grass.

Does weight training regularly throughout the winter and early track season. Weight training is concentrated on upper body development, but also does leg work. Coached by C. Trehearne and G. Gowan. Runs in meets twice per week in early season and slacks off to one race per week by late season. AAA junior 220y champ in 1957. Set British record for 400m. with 45.9 in 1961. Won World Games 400m. in 1961.

Robbie Brightwell captured the 1962 European Championships 400 in 45.9. He was runner-up in the British Empire Games that year also and was ranked second in the world. At Tokyo he was captain of the British Olympic team. His lifetime best 45.7 was good for fourth place in the 400, but his brilliant 44.8 anchor leg brought Great Britain the silver medal in the 1600m. relay.

Robbie
Brightwell

Frank Budd

FRANCIS JOSEPH BUDD, Asbury Park (N.J.) H.S., Villanova University. Age 22, 1961.

BEST MARKS: 300 yards, 29.4; 220 yards, 20.2; 200m., 20.7; 100m., 10.2; 100 yards, 9.2 (world record); 60 yards, 6.1 seconds.

PERSONAL STATISTICS: Born July 20, 1939 at Long Beach, New Jersey. 5'11", 172 lbs.

PRE-RACE WARM-UP: Jog 880 yards. 10 minutes calisthenics. 3x150y at ½, ¾, and 9/10 full effort respectively. Walk briefly after each. 3x15 yards sprint starts from blocks.

TRAINING DURING NOVEMBER, 1961: Prior to each of the following workouts, warm-up with 1½ miles jogging, 15 minutes calisthenics, and 3-4x150 yards, starting at ½ effort and increasing speed of each. Monday: 20x220 yards in 28-31. Walk 220 yards after each. Tuesday and Friday: 10x440 yards in 72. Jog 440 yards in 3½ minutes after each of the first 5. Walk 440 yards after each of the last 5. Wednesday: 5x660 yards in 1:42-1:45. Walk 660 yards after each of the first 3. Walk 880 yards after the 4th 660 yards. Thursday: 25x220 yards in 28-31. Walk 220 yards after each. Saturday and Sunday: Rest.

WINTER TRAINING (February, 1961): Most of this training is on an outdoor banked board (wood) track, 12 laps per mile, or 146-2/3 yards per lap. Prior to each of the following workouts, warm-up with 880 yards jogging, 10 minutes calisthenics, and 6x75 yards at ¾ full effort, jogging 70 yards after each. Monday: 4x293.3 yards in 35. Walk 3-5 minutes after each. 6x75 yards at 9/10 full effort from running start. Jog and walk alternately 70 yards after each. Jog 440 yards. 6-10 sprint starts indoors on gymnasium floor, sprinting first 10 yards, and decelerating 30 yards on each. Tuesday: 660 yards in 1:32. Walk 5-10 minutes. 2x293.3 yards in 35. Walk 3-5 minutes after each. 6x75 yards at 9/10 full effort from running start. Jog and walk 70 yards after each. Jog 440 yards. 6 sprint starts indoors as on Monday. Wednesday: 15x75 yards at ¾ full effort from running start. Jog and walk 70 yards after each. Thursday: Rest if racing indoors on Friday. If racing on Saturday, then 6x75 yards from running start at ¾ full effort, with 70 yards walking and jogging after each. Friday and Sunday: Rest. Saturday: Indoor competition at 60 yards.

SUMMER TRAINING (May, 1961): Prior to each of the following workouts, warm-up with 1½ miles jogging, 15 minutes calisthenics, and 3-4x150 yards, starting at ½ effort and increasing speed of each. Monday: 660 yards in 1:25. Walk 5-10 minutes. 10x150 yards near full speed, from running start. Walk 150 yards after each. 300 yards in 32.5. Tuesday: 4x300 yards in 31-32.5. Walk 10-15 minutes after each. Wednesday:

6x150 yards from starting blocks. Walk 3-5 minutes after each. 20x35 yards sprint starts. Thursday: Rest if racing on Friday. If racing Saturday, 6x150 yards at ¾ full effort from running start. Walk 150 yards after each. Friday and Sunday: Rest. Saturday: Competition at 100 and 220 yards.

Most of the above workouts end with 440 yards of jogging as a warm-down, and 15 minutes of weight training, using a general weight program but concentrating on leg presses and toe raises using a "press machine" type apparatus.

In Budd's sprint starting position, his left starting block is 18" behind the starting line, and his right block is 34" behind the line. In the "set" position, he applies firm pressure on the rear block with his right foot, although most of his body weight is distributed evenly between the left foot and hands.

Budd starts pre-competitive training in late September. Indoor competition begins in early January and ends in mid-March. He rests one week at the end of indoor competition. His outdoor competitive season ends in late June, except in the event he tours abroad, in which case he continues competition until late July. He participates in 8-10 indoor meets and 10 outdoor meets annually in the USA. Budd rests one day prior to competition, and last eats 2-3 hours before racing. He is coached by James (Jumbo) Elliott and James Tuppeny, was a member of the 1960 U.S. Olympic team, placing fifth in the 100, and holds numerous American IC4A, NCAA, and AAU sprint titles.

Frank Budd

14

George Daniels

GEORGE KOFI BO DANIELS, University of Colorado, Boulder, Colorado. Age 21 years, 1971.

BEST MARKS: 440y, 46.9; 400m., 45.9e; 330y, 33.8t; 300m., 30.4e; 200m., 20.6; 220y, 20.4; 100m., 10.0; 100y, 9.2.

PERSONAL STATISTICS: Born April 9, 1950 at Takoradi, Ghana. 5'10", 160 lbs. Started racing in 1959 at age 9.

PRE-RACE WARM-UP: "I always like to spend much time jogging slow for my muscles to be loosened properly in order to stretch well. I personally feel that this is the best method to warm-up because you don't force the muscles to (become too loose too quick) and it prevents injuries." SUMMARY: 7-8 minutes mile run, 12-13 minutes stretching.

PRE-TRAINING WARM-UP: Same as Pre-Race.

WINTER TRAINING (Morning workouts at 9:00 AM, afternoon at 3:30 PM): Monday—PM, Warm-up, starts from blocks, 6x110 straights (walk curve for recovery) at ¾ speed stressing high knee lift. 1 mile jog warm-down. Tuesday—AM, Lift weights. PM, Warm-up, weights, 2x330 in 36-38 seconds (45 seconds rest between), 1x220 in 25-26 seconds (45 seconds rest after 330's). Wednesday—AM, Same as Tuesday. PM, Warm-up, 10 block starts, 10x110 straights at ¾ speed (walk curve for recovery). Thursday—AM, Same as Tuesday. PM, 2x550 (first 440 in 50 seconds), 1x220 at about 25 seconds. Friday—AM, Same as Tuesday. PM, Warm-up, 6x150 (jog 70y between). Saturday—AM, No workout. PM, Warm-up, 6x220 (30 seconds recovery). Sunday—AM, Jog 2-3 miles, 15-20 minutes stretching.

SPRING/SUMMER TRAINING (Morning workouts at 9:00 AM, afternoon at 3:30 PM): Monday: Same as WINTER schedule plus; 1x550, 1x440, 1x330, 1x220 with 30 seconds rest between. Tuesday-Sunday: Same as WINTER schedule.

WEIGHT PROGRAM: My weight lifting program consists of exercises for the lower and upper body regions. For upper body I do military press, bench press, etc. (3 sets of 10 reps each). For lower body, the exercises include leg raises, leg press, hamstring exercises, quadricep extensions, situps and quarter squats, etc. (again, 3 sets of 10 reps each).

Daniels, African record holder in the short sprints, competes in 15 indoor races and 25 outdoor meets annually. His rapid improvement since 1970 has gained him recognition nationally at Colorado, as well as in Big 8 and USTFF competition. Utilizing an elongated start, George sets his blocks 1 foot apart with a distance of 2'3" between front block and starting line. He does not rest the day before a meet, but does no training the morning of the race. George Daniels has been coached by the following men: Mr. J.E.A. Mills (Ghana), John Malcolm and Bill MacCarthy (U.S. Peace Corps), and Don Meyers (C.U.).

Otis Davis

OTIS C. DAVIS, University of Oregon. Age 28, 1960.

BEST MARKS: 400m., 44.9 (World and Olympic record); 330 yards, 31.8; 220 yards, 21.0; 200m., 20.9; 100m., 10.7; 100 yards, 9.6.

PERSONAL STATISTICS: Born July 12, 1932 at Tuscaloosa, Alabama. 6'2", 165 lbs. Started racing in 1958 at age 26.

PRE-RACE WARM-UP: Jog 10-15 minutes. 5-10 minutes calisthenics. 3-4x110-120 yards at half-effort. Spring 150 yards. Walk for recovery after each. Rest 5 minutes. Get up and jog easily until race. Duration of warm-up, 30-45 minutes.

WINTER TRAINING (January-February, 1960): Monday: (1) 5-15 minutes easy jogging. Easy calisthenics. (2) 10 minutes of short runs using slow, deliberate strides, bringing knees as high as possible to chest while still maintaining good form. (3) "Fast leg work." Bouncing or pattering the feet off the ground, lifting the feet only a short distance off the ground, and moving the feet as quickly as possible, working the arms in coordination with the legs. (4) Either (a) 4-6 starts from blocks at ¾ full speed, or (b) 4-12x100 yards sprints, reaching top speed at 50 yards, and decelerating the next 50 yards. Walk for recovery between. (5) Jog 5-10 minutes. Tuesday, Thursday, Saturday, and Sunday: (1) Weight training involving a series of lifting which exercises most of the major muscle groups, using half maximum weight capacity for each lift. Then 15 minutes easy jogging. Wednesday: (1) Jog 5-15 minutes. Easy calisthenics. (2) 4x110 yards in 12.5-13 seconds each, reaching full speed at 60 yards and sustaining full striding speed over final 50 yards of each. Walk for recovery after each. As season progresses, increase speed and number to maximum of 10 repetitions. (3) 15 minutes fartlek (speed-play) consisting of steady running, sprint 50 yards, walking, 300-500 yards fast striding, 50 yards sprint, and easy jogging. Friday: (1) Jog 5-15 minutes. Easy calisthenics. (2) High knee running as in (2) on Monday. (3) Fast leg work as in (3) on Monday. (4) 300-350 yards at 7/8 full effort. Walk for recovery. (5) 200-250 yards at 7/8 full speed. Walk for recovery. (6) 2-4x110 yards sprints.

SUMMER TRAINING (May, 1960): Monday: (1) Jog 5-15 minutes. Easy calisthenics. (2) 500 yards at 60 seconds 440 yards speed. Walk for recovery.

(3) 2-3x110 yards sprints. Recovery walk between. (4) 5-15 minutes fartlek. Tuesday: (Same as Tuesday during Winter training). Wednesday: (1) Jog 5-15 minutes. Easy calisthenics. (2) 8-12x110 yards sprints, or 4-6x220 yards at racing speed. Walk for recovery between. (3) 5-10 minutes easy jogging. Thursday and Friday: Jog 15 minutes. Easy calisthenics. Occasionally a few starts. Very easy. Saturday: Competition. Sunday: Rest.

Prior to 1958, Davis was a basketball player. Coached by Bill Bowerman, the 1960 Olympic 400m. champion's competitive season at the University of Oregon starts in April and ends in June. He participates in 6-15 meets annually. He begins preparation for track season in October. His workouts are taken in mid-afternoon, and are usually 60-90 minutes each. His starting blocks are 19 inches and 34 inches respectively from the starting line. Davis rests two days prior to major competition, and eats his last meal 3-5 hours prior to competition.

His tactics in the 400m. race involve a moderate start, full sprint stride to the 200m. mark, coasting or floating to the middle of the last turn, and accelerating to full effort for the finishing tape.

Otis Davis

Jim Green

JAMES LEE GREEN, Philadelphia Pioneer Club and University of Kentucky. Age 24, 1971.

BEST MARKS: Mile, 4:55; 880y, 1:59; 660y, 1:19.8; 440y, 47.1; 220y, 20.8; 100m., 10.0; 100y, 9.1.

PERSONAL STATISTICS: Born September 28, 1947 at Eminence, Kentucky. 5'11", 160 lbs. Started racing in 1963 at age 15.

PRE-RACE AND PRE-TRAINING WARM-UP: Jog approximately one mile. 5-10 minutes calisthenics. 4-8x110y acceleration sprints. Walk recovery after each.

FALL TRAINING: Monday: 6-8 miles slow, continuous running on roads. Tuesday: 7-9 miles easy running on grass with teammates. Wednesday: One hour continuous run, alternately jogging, sprinting, fast striding, and walking. Thursday: 6-9 miles road run at easy speed over hilly route. Friday: 90 minutes continuous activity as on Tuesday.

WINTER TRAINING: Monday: 10x660y in 1:40-1:42. Walk 660y after each. Tuesday: 10-12x150y in 17-18 seconds. Walk 220y after each. Wednesday: 10x440y in 68-72 seconds. Walk 440y after each. Thursday: 10-15x70y sprints from blocks. Walk return recovery after each. Friday: 1-2x(4x220y sprints). Walk 220y after each. Walk 440y between sets. Sometimes this is followed by baton exchanging practice with teammates. Saturday & Sunday: Rest.

SPRING/SUMMER TRAINING: Monday: 10x300y in 37 seconds. Walk 300y after each. Tuesday: 3x(4x150y in 16 seconds. Walk 150y after each). Walk 440y between sets. Wednesday: 2x(4x330y in 40 seconds. Walk 330y after each). Walk 880y between sets. Thursday: 3x(5x110y from running start. Walk 110y after each). Walk 330y between sets. First set is run in 11.5, the second in 11.0, and the final set in 10.5 seconds. Friday: Rest for Saturday's race. If there is no race on Saturday, run 2x(4x220y in 24 seconds each). Walk 880y between sets. Sunday: Rest.

Green never trains more than once daily. He uses weight training Monday, Wednesday, and Friday during the fall and winter. His front starting block is placed 12 inches behind the starting line. The rear starting block is placed 14 inches behind the front block. Green has been coached by Charlie Quertermous, Lloyd Block, and Press Whelan. He ran 9.5 in high school and at Kentucky was the USTFF 100 and 120 champion in both 1968 and 1970. In 1971 he was second in the AAU and USA-USSR meets and ranked third in the world in the 100.

Armin Hary

ARMIN HARY, age 23 years, 1960.

BEST MARKS: 200m., 20.5; 100m., 10.0 (WR); 70m. 7.5i (ER).

PERSONAL STATISTICS: Born March 22, 1937.

Armin Hary's seasonal training schedule was divided up into five separate periods: November-December, January-February, March-April, May-June, and July. The purpose of the first three divisions was for conditioning, increasing muscular power, and developing neuromuscular coordination. The May to June period was devoted to form building, and training after July for preservation of form.

NOVEMBER-DECEMBER TRAINING: (Six training days a week alternating easy with difficult workouts. 3½ times indoors with the remaining 2½ days outdoors. The indoor facility was a 50m. long hall.) Day 1: (Indoors) a) Warm-up consisting of 20 minutes running and exercises. b) Easy acceleration runs (30-40m.x10-12 at ¾ speed) 1 minute recovery interval. Emphasis was placed on smooth and relaxed running. c) 15-20x20-25m. easy starts. d) 10 minutes walk rest (to stay warm). Strength exercises: threw a medicine ball towards the ceiling 20x from a trunk bent forward position. After a short rest do 10 pushups of the medicine ball from the right and left side. (Duration, 10 minutes.) e) Walk recovery. f) Jumping exercises: from a crouched starting position hop over 8 low (30") hurdles placed 3m. apart; alternate feet when negotiating each jump. (Duration, 10 minutes.) g) 10-12 minutes handball, jogging. Day 2: (Outdoors) on grass. a) 25 minutes jogging and exercise warm-up. b) 8-10x80-100m. acceleration runs; 100-150m. easy walk recovery. Emphasis on "sharp tempo" and relaxed movements. c) 10-12 minutes walk rest. d) Easy runs of 200, 300, 400, and 200m. Day 3: (Indoors) a) Regular 25 minutes warm-up. The rest of the workout is the same as Day 1 except the medicine ball is replaced by a 30-40kg barbell and the exercises are performed for body-building. Also the 30" hurdles are raised to 36". Day 4: (Outdoors and indoors) a) Easy outdoor running for 30-45 minutes. b) Strength training similar to that of Day 1 with emphasis on short "intensive" movements. Day 5: (Indoors) one hour. Varied exercises including handball, medicine ball or barbell work, jogging, jumping, and starting may be used on this day. Day 6: (Outdoors) a) 1½ hours cross-country. b) Starting exercises.

JANUARY-FEBRUARY TRAINING: In these months the training is carried out in the same indoor-outdoor sequence as the previous month's schedule, but the training-burden is raised. The running tempo is sharper, the barbell is increased to 60kg, the number of medicine ball "up-throws" and push-ups is increased (20x with *both* hands. 10x push-ups with right and left hands).

MARCH-APRIL TRAINING: Due to better weather conditions, training is done outdoors 4x a week while indoor training goes on twice a week. From the beginning of April most of the workouts are out-of-doors. In March the weight lifting training is excluded. Day 1: (About the first week of April) a) 30 minutes jogging and exercise warm-up. b) Jumping and springing exercises on grass. c) Recovery walk. d) "tripplings"—fast runs with short but relaxed movements (6-8x30m.). e) Recovery walk. f) 6-8x120m. (12.0/100m. pace), walk for recovery. g) Easy runs of 200m., 300m., 200m., and 200m., h) Jogging. Day 2: a) Jogging and exercises. b) Starting exercises: 12-15x 30-35m. c) 6x150m. (12.5/100m. pace), walk for recovery. d) 10-15 easy crouch starts of 25-30m. e) Strength exercises: medicine ball, jumping, light weights, and exercises with shot. f) 4-5x150m. acceleration runs (last 60m. at 7/8 speed). g) Long jog. Day 3: a) running, throwing, and jumping exercises (depending on his disposition). b) 4x200m. in 25-26 seconds (200m. recovery walk). c) "Long duration" jogging. Day 4: a) Jogging and exercises. b) 3-4x120m. acceleration runs (walk back recovery). c) "tripplings" 5-6x40m. d) 10-15x25-30m. easy crouch starts. e) Strength exercises: medicine ball, jumping, and exercises with shot. f) 4-5x150m. acceleration runs with last 60m. at 7/8 speed. g) Long jog. Day 5: (Same as Day 3). Day 6: a) Jogging and exercises. b) cross-country. c) flying 60m. and 100m. runs stressing smoothness and relaxation. d) 30-45m. starts (quality not quantity stressed). e) Jogging.

MAY-JUNE TRAINING: Day 1: a) Jogging and exercises. b) 4-5 easy "tripplings" over 40-50m. c) 2-3 acceleration runs of 120-150m. d) 3 easy and 3 "sharp" 40m. starts. e) 3x50m. (flying start) in 5.0-4.8 (later in the season the time should be in the 4.8-4.6 seconds range). f) Flying 100m. dash (in the beginning of the training period the time is about 10.0, later on marks of 9.3 and 9.4 are recorded). g) 2x200m. in 23.0 seconds, walk for full recovery. h) Jogging. Day 2: a) Jogging and exercises. b) Easy medicine ball and jumping exercises (for maintaining strength). c) Easy starts, acceleration runs depending on the runner's disposition. d) Jogging. Day 3: a) Jogging and exercises. b) 3x120-150m. acceleration runs with walking recovery. c) Easy starts. d) 2x50m. all-out start. e) 3x50m. timed flying runs. f) 2x100m. flying runs. g) 1-3x220m. runs (23.0/200m. pace). Day 4: (If Hary had no scheduled meet during the week, the following workout would take place): a) Jogging and exercises. b) 3x150 acceleration runs, with walking recovery. c) 3 "tripplings" at full power, but with smoothness and relaxation of movement. d) 3 easy starts of 35-40m. e) 2x50m. gun starts. f) 2x100m. (easy first 50m., full power last 50m.). g) 1x50m. flying run, 1x60m. full power run, 1x100m. flying run, walking recovery between each.

JULY-ON TRAINING: The training schedules for individual workouts during the "big meet" part of the season were varied and dependent upon a variety of factors. If Hary felt that a certain competition coming up required a greater amount of, say, form work, more time would be devoted to this task. In summary, the most important modifications of Hary's training schedule were these: a) The number of runs, starts, and acceleration sprints were reduced. b) The speed of the runs remained the same. c) The number of training days remained the same. d) The recovery interval between runs is increased.

Armin Hary is best known for his 100m. victory in the 1960 Rome Olympics, and his former world record for that event of 10.0. But a unique and controversial type of starting position may live on as his most memorable accomplishment. Bud Winter, former head track coach of world class sprinters at San Jose State College in California, authored a book titled THE ROCKET SPRINT START. In that book he analyzed the unusually quick start and block placement of Armin Hary. The distance from starting line to front block was 23 inches, while a measurement of 10 inches separated the front from back block. The greatest point of interest in this starting position is the extremely low angle of lean as the runner leaves the starting blocks. With an aggressive and powerful drive of both arms, Hary was able to manage a very long first stride out of the blocks. Inspection of films at the 100m. final at the 1960 Olympics showed that Hary seemed to have a slight advantage over every other runner at the second stride (where slight advantages are rare). Because of the unusual speed in which Hary cleared the blocks, many starters were prone to call a false start. In fact, the starter was the one at fault; he could not accept an inordinately fast start!

Armin Hary leads the pack.

21

Gary Holdsworth

GARY ALFRED HOLDSWORTH, East Melbourne Harriers, Australia. Age 26 years, 1968.

BEST MARKS: 100y, 9.3; 100m., 10.3; 220y, 20.9; 200m., 20.9.

PERSONAL STATISTICS: Born January 8, 1942 at Coburg, Victoria, Australia. 5'9½, 172 lbs.

PRE-RACE WARM-UP: Jog 1-1½ miles or until feeling sufficiently warm. Exercises. 2 easy run-throughs (¾ pace). 2-3 starts.

PRE-TRAINING WARM-UP: Jog 1-1½ miles, exercises and 4-5 run-throughs (¾ pace).

WINTER TRAINING: Consists mainly of non-competitive cross-country running and repetition sprints. Cross-country runs of 2-3 miles are done 3 nights a week. Sundays are often used for repetitive 150y or 440y.

SUMMER TRAINING: The following training is used by Holdsworth for both early-season and competitive season. Monday: 4x150y (¾ speed). Wind sprints. Tuesday: 1x300y and 2x250y accelerations. Wednesday: 4-8 starts. 2 laps of wind sprints (sprinting the straights). Thursday: Some starts. 1 lap of wind sprints. 1x150y acceleration and 2-3x60y fast. Friday: Rest. Saturday: Competition. Sunday: Jog.

Before important meets commence Holdsworth participates in as many competitions as possible. Summer training sessions last 1½-2 hours. Coached by Neville Sillitoe.

Mike Larrabee

MIKE LARRABEE, Ventura (California) High School, University of Southern California, and Southern California Striders. Age 32, 1965.

BEST MARKS: 880y, 1:56.1; 660y, 1:17; 440y, 46.1; 400m., 44.9 (equals world record); 330y, 32.4; 220y, (curve) 21.0, (straightaway) 20.6; 100m., 10.5; 100y, 9.6.

PERSONAL STATISTICS: Born December 2, 1933 at Los Angeles, California. 6'1", 174 lbs. Started racing in 1949 at age 15. Retired from racing at age 32.

PRE-RACE WARM-UP: Jog ¾ to 1 mile in approximately 10 minutes.

3-4x100-150 yards at ¾ full speed, sprinting 25 yards on finish of final run. Walk 110 yards after each.

PRE-TRAINING WARM-UP: Jog 1 mile in 10 minutes. If workout is to include distances below 330 yards, run 3-4x110 yards at ¾ full speed. Walk 110 yards after each.

WINTER TRAINING: Start about December 20 annually. Racing season starts in May and ends about June 20 each year, unless competing abroad during July. No training between the end of racing season and approximately December 20.

TRAINING DURING RACING SEASON: Monday: 10x120 yards on grass with running start. Not timed, as fast as possible. Walk 120 yards after each. Tuesday: 2-3x220 yards from blocks as fast as possible under training conditions. Walk 440 yards after each. Time, usually faster than 23.0. Wednesday: 2x330 yards as fast as possible. Walk 880 yards between. Time, usually near 33.0-34.0. Thursday, Friday, and Sunday: Rest. Saturday: Race. Training prior to start of racing season (December 20 to May): Almost identical to racing season training, except for time-trial on Friday at 330, 440, or 660, plus 1-2x660 yards as fast as possible on Saturday.

Mike
Larrabee

Mike Larrabee

Larrabee's workouts lasted from 1 to 2 hours, starting at 3:00 PM. He never trained more than once daily, and did not use weight training. His last meal is eaten 4 hours prior to competition. He raced 2-5 times indoors and 20-30 times outdoors annually. In terms of competitive 440 yards tactics, he sprinted the first 50 yards, ran maximum speed with minimum tension from 50 yards to the 220 yards point, and attempted to kick the final 220 yards. He was coached by Jack Smith, Jess Mortensen, and Chuck Coker. His greatest athletic achievement was the 1964 Olympic gold in 400m.

Hardee McAlhaney

WINBON HARDEE MCALHANEY, JR. University of Tennessee. Age 20, 1967.

BEST MARKS: 880y, 1:54.0; 660y, 1:17.0; 440y, 46.1; 330y, 33.8; 220y, 21.9; 100y, 9.9.

PERSONAL STATISTICS: Born June 12, 1947 at Beaufort, South Carolina. 5'11", 160 lbs. Started racing in 1961 at age 14.

PRE-RACE WARM-UP: 880y jog, stretching, 440y jog, more stretching, 2x220y stride, 440y walk, 2-3x150y sprints, 2-3 starts, 15 minutes rest before race.

PRE-TRAINING WARM-UP: 880y jog, stretching and calisthenics.

FALL CROSS-COUNTRY TRAINING: Monday: 3-5x550y in 75 seconds or 3-5x660y in 1:35 plus several 110y strides. Tuesday: 2-5 miles of fartlek. Wednesday: 8-12x220y in 29-32 seconds. Thursday: 2-5 miles of fartlek. Friday: 6-10x330y in 42-45 seconds. Saturday: striding and calisthenics. Sunday: rest.

WINTER TRAINING: Monday: 4-6x550y passing 330y in 45 seconds and sprinting final 220y, 8x110y striding. Tuesday: 6-10x220y in 26-29 seconds and 8x110y striding. Wednesday: 4-8x330y in 36-39 seconds and 8x110y striding. Thursday: 2x(660y in 1:30, 440y in 58 seconds, 330y in 38 seconds and 220y in 25 seconds.) Friday: 15-25x110y fast, or if no meet easy striding. Saturday: race or easy striding. Sunday: rest.

SPRING TRAINING: Workouts Monday through Wednesday begin with start practice and baton work. Monday: 550y full speed, 2-4x550y passing 330y in 42 seconds and sprinting final 220y, 8-10x110y fast. Tuesday: 2x220y full speed, 2-4x220y in 22-23 seconds, 8x150y fast. Wednesday: 3-5x330y in 35-36 seconds plus several 110y striding. Thursday: fast striding. Friday: rest. Saturday: race. Sunday: 1-2 miles of jogging.

As a senior at Beaufort High School, McAlhaney won three South Carolina prep titles: 100y, 220y and 440y, the 440 in a record 48.2 seconds. At Tennessee he was Southeast Conference 440 champion. Weight training three times per week included bench press, arm curl, and "butterflies". He was coached by Frank Small and Chuck Rohe. Summer workouts consisted of a twice-weekly two-mile jog.

McAlhaney had a 45.7 400m. in 1968.

Fanahan McSweeney

JOHN FANAHAN McSWEENEY, McNeese State University (Lake Charles, Louisiana) and Ireland. Age 24 years, 1971.

BEST MARKS: 880y, 1:51.6 (1:48.5 relay); 440y, 46.3; 220y, 21.1; 100y, 9.5.

PERSONAL STATISTICS: Born November 25, 1947 in County Cork, Ireland. 6' (1.83 meters), 168 lbs. (76 kilograms). Started racing in 1957 at age 10.

PRE-RACE WARM-UP: Jog ½-¾ mile, stride 4-5x150y, relax for 15 minutes, 10 minutes before race a few easy strides and stretching exercises.

PRE-WORKOUT WARM-UP: Jog ¼-½ mile, stride 1x220y, stretching exercises.

FALL TRAINING: McSweeney does a morning workout of 8 miles (7 minutes pace) on the flats of a golf course, Monday through Thursday. Monday: 6x1 mile on road (5 minutes rest between) @ 5:10. Tuesday: 8x880y @ 2:20, 10-12 mile cross-country run. Wednesday: 3 sets of 5x30sec-60 sec-90seconds runs, 7x880y @ 2:20. Thursday: 8-12 miles on road. Friday: 5-6 miles. Saturday: competition (4-6 miles). Sunday: (optional) 8-15 miles easy.

WINTER TRAINING: Monday: 4x330y @ 42 seconds, 4x660y @ 1:32. Tuesday: 16x220y @ 27 seconds. Wednesday: 10-12 mile cross-country run @ 5:20 pace. Thursday: 8-12 miles easy. Friday: (competition on Saturday) 5-8 miles, (no competition) 440y-550y-660y-770y-880y and back to 440y @ 63-65 440y pace (2 minutes rest between). Saturday: competition (if none, 10-12 miles fartlek). Sunday: rest or jog 5-10 miles.

SPRING/SUMMER TRAINING: McSweeney does a morning workout of 4 miles, Monday through Thursday. Monday: 2x330y below 40 seconds (2½ minutes rest between), rest 5 minutes, 2x660y below 1:29 (5 minutes rest between) or 2x¾ mile @ 3:12-3:15 (20 minutes rest between), 1x660t all out. Tuesday: 18-22x220y below 26.5 seconds (1½-2 minutes rest between). Wednesday: 8-12 mile cross-country run @ 5:40 pace. Thursday: 16-20x150y @ 17.5 seconds (1½-2 minutes rest between). Friday: 4-6 miles. Saturday: competition. Sunday: 10-18 miles.

The distances from starting to front block and between blocks, utilized by McSweeney, are 15 in. and 7 in. respectively. Coached by Robert Hayes at McNeese State, he holds the Irish national record for 100y, 220y, 440y and is European record holder for 440y indoors.

McSweeney represented Eire at the 1972 Olympic Games in Munich and ran a non-qualifying 47.07 in his 400m. heat.

Adrian Metcalfe

ADRIAN METCALFE, Oxford University A.C., Leeds A.C., England, Achilles. Age 19 years, 1961.

BEST MARKS: (as of Nov. 1961) 440y, 46.4; 400m., 45.7; 200m., 21.3; 100y, 9.8.

PERSONAL STATISTICS: Born March 2, 1942 at Bradford, Yorkshire, England. 6'2'', 174 lbs. Started racing in 1956 at age 14.

TRAINING: "I go out virtually every day (not immediately prior to competition), winter and summer. I do nothing but run, with the emphasis on quality running. Everything must be done fast and relaxed. Thus in summer: Monday: 3x330y (34.0), 1x220y (22.0); Tuesday: 9x150y (14.5) . . . and so forth. Winter embodies more stamina work: 6x220y (23.0)—but still fast. In fact I can't say much about training methods, since I make them up each day when I go out. I find training on my own all the time has given me much greater mental strength ('guts' if you like) and that is just as important as physical grind. If I feel I'm really hurting myself in training (the actual times and distances are unimportant) my mind and body become accustomed to keeping moving when sanity demands I give up."

Metcalfe did a little circuit training during the winter but no weights. He competed indoors as well as outdoors and credits his 60y dash races in helping him prepare for the outdoor campaign. Along with numerous dual meet wins between England and other European countries, Adrian held U.K. and European records in the 400m. and 440y. *Track and Field News* ranked him first in the world for his events as a 19-year-old. Metcalfe's form has its bad points (an idiosyncrasy of running with legs out sideways), but he considers his stride length (which reaches up to 9'6'') an asset.

Adrian Metcalfe, after handing off to Robbie Brightwell.

Curtis Mills

Curtis Mills

CURTIS MILLS, Texas A&M. Age 21, 1970.

BEST MARKS: 880 yards, 1:56 high school; 440 yards, 44.6 (r), 44.7 (WR), 220 yards, 20.6 turn, 19.6 (r).

PERSONAL STATISTICS: Born October 6, 1948. 6'4", 175 lbs.

PRE-RACE WARM-UP: Warm-up for and use the sprint relay for race preparation. Runs until he feels a little tired with a good sweat. This he feels keeps his neck, shoulders and arms from tightening in the first 110 or 220 of the race.

PRE-TRAINING WARM-UP: Six repeat 100's and then right into the schedule.

TRAINING: Mills training is divided into three phases. Phase one is the early season and is devoted to the development of stamina and overall conditioning by using the up and down the ladder method with the emphasis on volume at a slower pace. Up and down the ladder running is on a Tartan track and the longer run is on the roads. Monday: For the first six to eight weeks of training he runs 3¼ miles. By the last week he runs it in about 21 minutes. After this period Monday returns to the regular schedule as shown below.

EARLY SEASON: Monday/Tuesday: choose one of the below—emphasis volume at slower pace. 1) 220-220-660-220-220-440-220-220. 2) 110-110-220-220-660 or 550-220-220-110-110. 3) 110-110-330-330-550-330-110-110. 4) 220-220-660-440-220 (Mills favorite workout). 5) 220-220-660-220-220-330-110-110. Wednesday/Thursday: choose one of the below—less volume and faster. 1) 220-220-550-220-220. 2) 110-110-220-330-220-110-110. 3) 110-110-110-110-330-330-110-110. 4) 330-220-110-110-220-330. In these workouts the times up the ladder are slower than the times down. Ex. 17.5, 17.5, 17.5, 35, 35, 52.5, 45, 33, 33, 15, 15 seconds. 110-110-110-220-220-330-330-220-220-110-110 yards. After two months, for an occasional break, seven-man 880 relays are run with each runner running 7 to 10 legs with each of the 220 legs at 28 to 30 seconds.

PRE-SEASON AND SEASON: The second phase of training (Jan.-Mar.) is the pre-season and season with a change to a 440 yard dash schedule. Emphasis is now on speed over a longer distance. Mills practices for relays and this running takes care of some of his shorter fast sprints. Monday: 2x500 (440 under 50), plenty of rest. Tuesday: 1x660 (about 1:21) or 2x660. Wednesday: 6x220 (slow pace about 30), day to recuperate. Thursday: 4 or 5x300 or 6-7x220. Friday: 5x220 or 8x150, 5 medium, 3 fast.

SEASON AND LATE SEASON: The third phase of training (April-June) is the season and late season training, which places an emphasis on faster runs over shorter distances with full recovery in between. Monday: 1x500 (440 fast), 2x150 fast. Tuesday: 3-4x300 (ave. 31.5 for four). Wednesday: 4x220 (ave. 22.0) or 6 step down 150's, 3 medium, 3 fast. Thursday: 5-6 step down 150's slow to fast or 5-6 100 yards with a flying start (Mills ave. 9.0 with a 10 yard flying start). Friday: Rest. Saturday: Rest. Monotony breakers or bad weather workouts: 1) 7-man continuous 880 relay (7-10x220). 2) In and out 110's (stride a 110, walk a 110—repeat). 3) 8-15 repeat 150's. 4) 8-12 repeat 220's.

JUNE: Monday—AM, 6x150 fast. PM, 6x110 fast. Tuesday—AM. 5x150 fast. PM, 5x220, 23.0 to 21.0. Wednesday—AM, 6x110 fast. PM, Easy warm-up only. Thursday—AM, 4x150 fast. PM, rest. Friday: rest. Saturday: ran 46.2 in National Fed. Meet. Sunday: rest. Monday: 4x150 fast. Tuesday: 4x150 fast. Wednesday: rest. Thursday: rest. Friday: 45.7 in the NCAA prelims. Saturday: 44.7 in the NCAA finals (WR).

In a race, Mills tries to run a good 220 and feel strong at this point, since the third 110 is the hardest for him. Time trials are run in early season only as a tune-up and as a check on progress. All of the interval work is done with a walk of the distance run following each run. Mills eats no special diet and feels that the three mile runs done at a decent pace (not a race) were most helpful in giving him the necessary foundation, confidence, and background while the 150's aided him in running relaxed. Weight training consists of situps and squats with light weights. Mills does not like to have a time limit imposed on a workout, he wants to take his time and not hurry the workout. His coach is Charles Thomas.

Bobby Morrow

BOBBY JOE MORROW, San Benito (Texas) High School and Abilene Christian College.

BEST MARKS: 440y, 46.6 (relay); 300y, 29.2; 220y, 20.4; 200m., 20.6 (curve); 100m., 10.2; 100y, 9.3 (equal world record).

PERSONAL STATISTICS: Born October 15, 1935 at Harlingen, Texas. 6'½", 175 lbs. Started racing in 1948 at age 12. Terminated racing career in 1960 at age 24.

PRE-RACE WARM-UP: Begin 45 minutes prior to race. Jog ½ to ¾ mile. 10 minutes calisthenics. 12-15x60-75 yards acceleration runs on grass, reaching near full speed at conclusion of each. Walk for recovery between.

Sprint 75 yards. 2-3 short starts from blocks. Rest 5 minutes before race.

PRE-TRAINING WARM-UP: Jog ¾ mile. 10 minutes calisthenics. Ground hurdling exercises.

WINTER TRAINING: (January, with first competition scheduled for the first week of March). Monday: 3 miles cross-country run on road. First 1½ miles at continuous, steady pace. Final 1½ miles alternately sprinting 75-150 yards and jogging 75-150 yards. Then 6-8x220 yards in 26-28 seconds. Walk 220 yards after each. Tuesday: 3-5x110 yards acceleration runs on grass, reaching ¾ full speed at end of each. Walk 110 yards after each. 5-10x30-50 yard sprint starts from blocks on grass at ½ to ¾ full effort. 4x220 yards on curve in 24-26: Walk 220 after each. Wednesday: If weather cold, repeat Monday's workout. If warm, run 2x300 yards in 33-35. Walk 5 minutes after each. 6-10x100 yards on grass at ¾ full speed, using high knee lift. Walk 100 yards after each. Thursday: Repeat Monday's training if weather cold. Otherwise, 440 in 58, 300 in 34, 220 in 25, and 110 in 11.5. Jog 440 yards after each. Friday: 2-3x100 yards acceleration runs using high knee lift, reaching 7/8 full speed at finish of each. Walk 100 yards after each. 2x300 yards in 31-32. Walk and jog 5 minutes between. Then 15 minutes walking and jogging, followed by 10x100 yards fast striding on grass. Walk 100 yards after each. Saturday: 10x30-50 yards sprint starts from blocks, using ¾ full effort on each. 4x220 yards on curve in 24-25. Walk 220 after each. Sunday: Rest. In addition to above, at least twice per week Morrow practiced baton exchanges with the sprint relay team at ½ to ¾ full sprinting effort for 15-30 minutes.

COMPETITIVE SEASON TRAINING: (April) Monday: 6-8x220 yards in 24-26. Walk 220 yards after each. Tuesday: 20 minutes baton exchanging practice, running 50 yards at ¾ full effort with each exchange. 10-12x30-40 yards sprint starts from blocks with gun. 2x220 yards on curve in 22-23. Walk 5 minutes between. Wednesday: 10 minutes baton exchange practice on grass. 3x150 yards in 14.5-15. Walk 5 minutes between. Thursday: 6-10x30-40 yards sprint starts from blocks at ½ to ¾ full effort. Walk back to starting line for recovery after each. 10-12x80-100 yards acceleration runs at ½ to ¾ full effort. Walk 80-100 yards after each. Friday: Rest, or 15 minutes alternately walking and striding, using high knee lift. Saturday: Competition. Sunday: Rest. Directly after each warm-up during competitive season training, Morrow spent 10 minutes running 6-8x80-100 yards acceleration runs on grass, using high knee lift, reaching ¾ to 7/8 full speed at end of each, and walking briefly for recovery between. All workouts were concluded with 10 minutes of easy warm-down jogging. Morrow's front and rear starting blocks were placed 18½ inches and 33 inches respectively behind the starting line. He was coached by Jake Watson and Oliver Jackson. Jackson and Morrow recognized that in sprinting form the runner's heel actually does make firm contact with the running surface for an instant during each sprinting stride, and that the body tends toward and upright position at full speed. During his final two competitive seasons, Morrow used weight training.

FALL TRAINING: Morrow ran cross-country with 2½ lbs. weights strapped to his ankles. He also used these ankle weights in running up and down the football stadium steps for 10-20 minutes, three times weekly during the Fall. Morrow never trained more than once daily. His workouts were approximately 90 minutes each, starting at 3:00 PM. He rested two days prior to competition in late competitive season. His last meal was eaten 3½ hours prior to racing, and he participated in approximately 15 meetings annually. His competitive season extended from March to July.

Winner of the James E. Sullivan award and holder of numerous National AAU and NCAA titles, Morrow won the 100 and 200 meters at the Melbourne Olympic Games in 1956. He was rated by Maxwell Stiles in his book *The Greatest Sprinters* as the greatest sprinter who ever lived.

Bobby Morrow

Wendell Mottley

WENDELL MOTTLEY, Yale University. Age 23, 1964.

BEST MARKS: 600y, 1:09.2 (WIR); 500y, 55.5 (=WIR); 440y, 45.8; 400m., 45.2; 220y, 21.0; TJ, 47'7" (14.50).

PERSONAL STATISTICS: Born July 12, 1941 in Trinidad. 5'11", 163 lbs.

PRE-RACE WARM-UP: 880 jog, stretching exercises, two or three 60y blasts.

TRAINING PROGRAM: Monday: 4x300y near maximum—10 minute interval. Tuesday: Repeat Monday's work. Wednesday: 5x440y—Relaxed but near maximum effort. Thursday: 1x600y (1:13), 1x440y (50.0), 1x300y (37.0). Friday: 3x(3x220y near full speed). Walk 4 minutes after each. Saturday: Repeat any of above. Sunday: Rest.

Mottley is coached by Robert Giegengack and Dr. Frank Ryan. He competes once per week and likes two days of rest before competing. Mottley trains at 3:00 PM for 1½-2 hours. At Tokyo, he won the Olympic silver medal in the 400m. At Yale, he was one of the finest indoor long sprinters of all-time, setting or equaling world bests from 440 to 600 yards.

Wendell
Mottley

Ira Murchison

IRA JAMES MURCHISON, Western Michigan University, Kalamazoo, Michigan, University of Chicago Track Club, Chicago, Illinois. Age 26 years, 1959.

BEST MARKS: 440, 49.0; 220, 20.4; 200m., 21.0 (t); 100m., 10.1; 100y, 9.3; 60y, 6.1; 50y, 5.1; 40y, 4.2.

PERSONAL STATISTICS: Born February 6, 1933 at Chicago, Illinois. 5'4", 135 lbs.

PRE-RACE WARM-UP: Jog 880, walk and jog a mile with calisthenics enroute, 10x150 accelerations, 300 at fast pace.

PRE-TRAINING WARM-UP: 15 minutes calisthenics, jog 6x120, stride 4x120 around curves.

FALL TRAINING: Monday-Friday: 10x150 from blocks in 15-16 seconds, 4x40 sprints from blocks.

WINTER TRAINING: Fall training is continued until racing condition is reached, then spring training is used.

SPRING TRAINING: Monday: 10x150 accelerations from blocks, walk 150 after each, 330y in 34 seconds, 10-25x25-50 starts from blocks. Tuesday:

Ira Murchison

Rest. Wednesday: 5x80 sprints from blocks, 6-7x110 fast striding, walk 110 after each. Thursday: Rest. Friday: Rest or competition. Saturday: Competition. Sunday: Rest.

Duration of workouts: At 4 PM for 2 hours. Participates in 30-40 indoor and 30-40 outdoor races a year. He equaled the world 100 yard record of 9.3 and set the global 100m. record at 10.1. In the 1956 100-meter final, Murchison placed fourth. He was also a member of the record-setting U.S. 400m. relay team. He has been coached by George Dales, Lloyd Williams, Hank Spring, Frank Koester, and Ted Haydon.

Paul Nash

PAUL NASH, University of Witwatersrand, South Africa. Age 22, 1969.

BEST MARKS: 400m., 46.1; 220y, 20.5; 200m., 20.1; 100m., 10.0; 100y, 9.2.

PERSONAL STATISTICS: Born January 20, 1947.

TRAINING: A seven week example of Paul Nash's training; 1st week: Monday: Weight program, 4x150y hill training at ¾ speed. Tuesday: 3x300m. in 37.0 seconds. Wednesday: Weight program, 4x150y hill running at ¾ speed. Thursday: 4x220y in 23.0 seconds. Friday: Weight program, 5x500y hill runs at full effort. Saturday: Rest. Sunday: Rest. 2nd week: Monday: Weight program, 5x150y at 7/8 speed. Tuesday: 3x220y in 22.0 seconds. Wednesday: Weight program, 5x150y at 7/8 speed. Thursday: 4-6 starts over 30y, 3xflying 50y. Friday: Rest. Saturday: Competition. 3rd week: Monday: Weight program, 3x300m. rhythm running on grass. Tuesday: 4x150y at 7/8 speed. Wednesday: Weight program, 4x150y fast downhill running. Thursday: 5-6 starts, 4xflying 50y. Friday: Weight program, 4x150y at 7/8 effort. Weekend: Rest. 4th week: Monday: Weight program, 3x200m. rhythm running. Tuesday: 2x300m. in 34.0 seconds. Wednesday: 4xflying 50y, 2x150y at 7/8 speed. Thursday: Weight program, 4x200m. steady running. Friday: 3x200m. in 22.0 seconds. 5th week: Monday: Weight program, 2x200m. in 24.0 seconds. Tuesday: 2x300m. in 34.0 seconds. Wednesday: 6x150y building up to maximum effort over last 70y. Thursday: Weight program, 150y downhill running at 7/8 speed. Friday: 2x200m. in 21.5 seconds. 6th week: Monday: Weights, 3x150y downhill running. Tuesday: 5x200m. in 21.5 seconds. Wednesday: 4x150y buildups, all-out last 90y. Thursday: 6-8 all-out starts over 50y. Friday: Weight training, 2x600-800y loose running on golf course. 7th week: Monday: Weights, jogging and 40 minutes stretching exercises on grass. Tuesday: 5x50y all-out starts. Wednesday: 1x300m. in

34.0 seconds, 1x200m. in 21.0 seconds, 2x100m. in 7/8 effort. Thursday: 5xflying 50y, 2 150y buildups. Friday: 5x50y all-out, loose running and stretching for 40 minutes.

WEIGHT PROGRAM: Rowing motion with dumbbells (2 sets of 7-12 reps.) Alternate bench press with dumbbells (2 sets of 7-12 reps.) Parallel squat with toe raise (squats combined with toe raise), (1 set of 7-12 reps). Knee raise with iron boot (2 sets of 7-12 reps.). Leg extension (2 sets of 7-12 reps.). Leg curl (2 sets of 7-12 reps.). Straight-leg dead lift (1 set of 10-15 reps.). Twisting sit-ups (1 set of 16-20 reps.). Bouncing split (1 set of 16-20 reps.). Side leg raise (2 sets of 7-12 reps.).

Nash holds records in both the short sprints for his native country. His renowned career in South Africa began with Junior championships in the same distances as his records. Paul's Air Force coach, John Short, brought Nash along with a combination of weight training and pure sprinting workout. Holding to the belief that "long slow distance" does not adequately prepare a sprinter for his event, Nash seldom ran at distances over 150 yards, but, as his training schedule shows, he is not adverse to running a fast 300m.

COMMENT FROM THE COACH: "I believe that fast running begets fast running. Sprinters should not indulge in long slow distance running. I also believe that full speed running should not be done more than three times a week, preferably on alternate days. Days in between can be spent doing rhythm running or hill running for maintenance of strength."

Peter Norman

PETER NORMAN, East Melbourne (Australia) Harriers Athletic Club. Age 26, 1968.

BEST MARKS: 400m., 46.9; 440 yards, 47.3; 200m., 20.0; 220 yards, 20.8; 100m., 10.3; 100 yards, 9.5.

PERSONAL STATISTICS: Born June 15, 1942 at Melbourne, Victoria. 5'10½", 166 lbs.

PRE-RACE WARM-UP: Jog 880, 220 walk, 440 jog, 220 walk, stretching exercises, 120 yards striding, four to six starts.

PRE-TRAINING WARM-UP: One mile jog, three 100 yards run-throughs.

WINTER TRAINING: Monday: warm-up, 10x100, 2x300. Tuesday: warm-up, 4x150, 1x300 yards in 7/8 pace. Wednesday: warm-up, 6x220 (:25).

Thursday: warm-up, 3x110, 3x330 (¾ speed), 4x150. Friday: rest. Saturday: three to four miles cross-country.

PRE-SEASON TRAINING: Monday: warm-up—sprint—jog—walk 440 yards, 1x300 yards (7/8 speed). Tuesday: warm-up, sprint—jog—walk 440 yards, 3x100 yards. Wednesday: warm-up, starts, 3x100, walk and jog 440, 3x100, walk and jog 440, 3x100. Thursday: warm-up, walk and jog 440, starts, 2x150, walk and jog 440, 2x60 yards. Friday: rest. Saturday: time trials. 100-220-440.

COMPETITIVE SEASON: Monday: warm-up, sprint—jog—walk 440, walk and jog 440, 2x300 yards. Tuesday: warm-up, starts, 2x150 on curve, walk and jog 440, 2x150 on straight. Wednesday: warm-up, sprint—jog—walk 440, starts, 3x100. Thursday: warm-up, sprint, jog, walk 440, starts, 3x60 yards on curve. Friday: rest. Saturday: competition. Sunday: rest.

Norman is coached by Neville Sillitoe. He won the 1968 Australian National championships with a fast 20.5. He later placed second at Mexico in 20.0, his personal best.

Ray Norton

OTIS RAY NORTON, San Jose State College, Oakland Junior College, and Oakland (California) High School. Age 22 years, 1959.

BEST MARKS: 220 yards, 20.2 seconds; 200m., 20.6 (curve); 100m., 10.1 seconds (=world record); 100 yards, 9.3 seconds (=world record).

PERSONAL STATISTICS: Born September 22, 1937 at Tulsa, Oklahoma. 6'2½", 180 lbs. Started racing in 1947 at age 10.

WARM-UP: (Identical for workout or competition). Jog 880 yards very slowly. Gymnastic exercises. 3x100y fast running, each faster than the previous one. 110 yards running concentrating upon lifting the knees high. Walk 110 yards after each 110 yards of running. 2-4x30 yards sprint starts, beginning slowly and increasing speed to fast start. Duration of warm-up—20 minutes.

PRE-COMPETITIVE (WINTER) SEASON TRAINING:Monday: 10x110 yards. Walk 110 yards after each. Start with 15 seconds each 110 yards, and reduce the time by one second each month until four weeks before competition. Following these 110-yards runs, run 440 yards, alternately sprint-

ing 15 yards and jogging 15 yards. Tuesday: Sprint starts. 2x20 yards. 2x30 yards. 2x40 yards. Then 5x220 yards. Walk 220 yards after each. Start at 32 seconds each and reduce the time by two seconds each month until four weeks before competition. Finally, ten minutes of baton exchanging practice with relay teammates. Wednesday: 5x55 yards. 5x110 yards. 5x55 yards. Walk an equal distance after each. The speed is identical to Monday, except that the 55 yards repetitions are slightly faster. Then finally 440 yards of alternately sprinting 15 yards and jogging 15 yards as on Monday. Thursday: 20 minutes of baton exchanging practice with relay teammates. Then 3x300 yards at ¾ full speed, sprinting at the finish. Walk 300 yards after each. Gradually reduce the time (increase the speed) of the 300 yards runs each week. Friday: 15 minutes of baton exchanging practice with teammates. Saturday: 2x60 yards sprints. Walk for full recovery. Then 300 yards as on Thursday. Sunday: Rest.

COMPETITIVE SEASON (SUMMER) TRAINING. Monday: 2x300 yards as on Thursday (above). Tuesday: Sprint starts. 2x20 yards, 2x30 yards. 2x40 yards. Walk an equal distance after each. Then 15 minutes of baton exchanging practice with relay teammates. Finally, 3-4x220 yards fast striding, but not timed. Walk 220 yards after each. Wednesday: 2x60 yards sprints. Walk 60 yards after each. 1-2x300 yards fast striding, but not timed. Walk 300 yards after each. Thursday: 15 minutes baton exchanging practice with relay teammates. 4-6 sprint start. Friday and Sunday: Rest. Saturday: Race.

Ray Norton

Duration of workouts: 1½ hours or less, starting at 3:00 PM daily. Competitive season extends from February to July, and extends until September in case of foreign athletic tours. Rests two months at end of competitive season, prior to beginning pre-competitive (Winter) training for coming season. Norton never trains more than once daily. He rests from one to two days prior to competition, and participated in 58 races during 1959. He prefers three hours between his final meal and the race. His front starting block is 16 inches from the starting line, and his rear starting block is 17 inches behind the front starting block. Norton's training also includes fun competition with teammates at hop-step-jumping, standing broad-jump, javelin throwing for accuracy, and left-hand shot-putting. He engages in light weight-training at the end of some of his workouts. Suffered fracture at base of right thumb playing football in High School which never healed properly. Consequently, in crouch sprint start he uses curled hand with knuckles on ground.

Norton placed sixth in both sprints in Rome in 1960.

Mel Patton

MELVIN E. PATTON, University of Southern California.

BEST MARKS: 220 yards, 20.2 (World record, 1949); 200m., 20.2 (World record, established 1949); 100m., 10.4; 100 yards, 9.3 (World record, established May 15, 1948).

PERSONAL STATISTICS: Born November 16, 1924. 6', 147 lbs. Started racing in 1939 at age 14. Terminated racing career in 1949 at age 24.

WARM-UP: (Identical for competition or workout). Jog 440 yards. 20 minutes of calisthenics. 8x110 yards acceleration runs, sprinting final 30 yards of last three. Walk 110 yards after each.

TRAINING: Essentially the same training was used, starting in January, and continuing to the end of the competitive season in June or July. Monday: 3x220 yards in 26.0; 25.5; and 25.0. Walk for recovery between. Occasionally this workout was replaced by one easy 220 yards (28-30), and one 330 yards at maximum effort. Tuesday: 6-10x20-40 yards sprint starts from blocks with gun. Walk directly back to starting line after each. 220 yards, sprinting first 50-75 yards, and "floating" remaining distance. One timed 150-175 yard sprint from blocks. Wednesday: 10-15x20-40 yards sprints with gun from blocks. 2x50 or 75 timed with sprints. Walk for recovery after each. Thursday: 6-8x20-40 yards sprint starts with gun. One

timed 50 yard sprint. Friday & Sunday: Rest. Saturday: Competition or time trial.

Coached by Kim Pursell, Dean Cromwell, and Jess Hill, Patton was 1948 Olympic 200m. champion. From the end of the competitive season in June or July until January, Patton took one or two workouts each week, somewhat similar to his warm-up, plus rope climbing. He did no weight training. Workouts lasted 90 minutes, starting at 3:00 PM. He never trained more than once daily, and participated in approximately 15 meetings per season. His last meal was eaten 2½-3 hours prior to competition. Patton started with his right foot forward, but never bothered to measure the distance between the blocks and the starting line, and changed these distances often. He was the first to run a 9.3 century.

In 1949 Patton ran a 9.1 hundred aided by a 6.5 followed wind. Several watches caught him in 9.0. In his book *The Greatest Sprinters* Maxwell Stiles suggests that here was the fastest 100 yards ever run by man.

Mel Patton

Bob Perry

ROBERT EARL PERRY, Lincoln High School, Port Arthur, Texas. Age 19 years, 1971.

BEST MARKS: 330y, 33.0; 300m., 30.6 (e); 220y, 21.0; 100m., 10.3 (e); 100y, 9.4.

PERSONAL STATISTICS: Born September 28, 1952 at Port Arthur, Texas. 5'11", 147 lbs. Started racing in 1966 at age 13.

PRE-RACE WARM-UP: Run 1 mile in 6 minutes, exercise, run 880y, walk 440y.

PRE-TRAINING WARM-UP: 3 mile run in 20 minutes. 6x100y warm-down following workouts.

FALL TRAINING: Monday, Tuesday, Wednesday, Thursday, and Friday—3 mile run. Saturday—1-2 mile run. Sunday—None.

WINTER TRAINING: Cross-country running Monday-Friday.

SPRING/SUMMER TRAINING: Monday—1x440y in 54 seconds; 1x220y in 23 seconds, 6x60y; 1x500y. Tuesday and Wednesday—1x440y in 54 seconds; 1x220y in 23 seconds; 6x60y; 3x220y. Thursday—Speed workout. Friday—Warm-up and warm-down. Saturday and Sunday—None.

In Perry's sprint starting position, his front starting block is 5" behind the starting line, and his rear block is 23" behind the line.

Coached by Vernon Wells, Cordell Lindsey, Carl Jackson, Leroy Leopold, and Joe Washington. Competes outdoors 36 times annually and indoors 5 times per year. 1971 Texas state sprint champion.

Julius Sang

JULIUS MARTIN SANG, North Carolina Central University (Durham, North Carolina) and Kenya. Age 24 years, 1972.

BEST MARKS: 6 miles, 40:00 (t); 2 miles, 13:00 (t) (e); 1 mile, 6:00 (t); 800m., 1:53; 660y, 1:30 (t); 400m., 44.9; 440y, 46.9; 300m., 33.2; 330y, 35.0 (t); 200m., 20.7; 220y, 20.4; 100m., 10.3; 100y, 9.3.

PERSONAL STATISTICS: Born September 19, 1948 at Kapsabet, Kenya. 5'9",

155 lbs. Started racing in 1960 at age 13.

PRE-RACE WARM-UP: Slow jogging up to 2 miles and strength exercises for total body development.

PRE-WORKOUT WARM-UP: Run up to 3 miles and muscle developing exercises.

COMPETITIVE SEASON: In Kenya there is but one season, Summer, and the competitive season encompasses the months of April through November for outdoor track and January through April for cross-country. Sang neither competes nor has a training program for the cross-country season. (April-November) Monday: 3x400m. @ 55 seconds (4 minutes jog between), 5x400m. @ ¾ speed, 2 mile warm-down. Tuesday: 100y @ 13 seconds, 220y @ 25 seconds, 330y @ 38 seconds, 550y @ 68 seconds, 330y @ 40 seconds, 220y @ 26 seconds, 110y @ 14 seconds. Wednesday: 5 miles on golf course in 36 minutes, 15 minutes warm-down. Thursday: speed work on grass at 150y distance @ 4/5 speed with clear emphasis on knee lifting and forward thrust in last 50y. Friday: 4x330y @ 38 seconds, ½ hour work with weights up to 250 lbs. Saturday: Progression from 110y to 330y and from 330y to 110y not timed but at reasonable pace, timed 500y @ 60 seconds. Sunday: no training.

Kenyan champion at 100y, 200y and 400m., Sang has been coached by John Velzian (in Kenya) and Dr. Leroy Walker (at North Carolina Central University). Sang finished third in the 1972 Olympic 400m. in a personal best 44.92. Then his electrifying 43.5 anchor leg in the 1600m. relay brought the Kenyan national team from behind to the gold medal. It was the best relay leg of the Games by .6 and the second fastest ever run.

Dave Sime

DAVID SIME, Duke University. Age 24 years, 1960.

BEST MARKS: 220 yards low hurdles, 22.2 (world record); 220 yards (straight), 20.0 (world record); 200m., (straight), 20.0 (world record); 100m., 10.2; 100 yards, 9.3 seconds (equals world record).

PERSONAL STATISTICS: Born July 25, 1936 at Patterson, New Jersey. 6'3", 176 lbs. Started racing in 1954 at age 19.

PRE-RACE WARM-UP: Begin 30 minutes before race. Jog easily for 15 minutes. Stride 220 to 330 yards "briskly." 4-6x20-30 yards starts, beginning easily and increasing the intensity of each. Then light calisthenics, walking, and jogging until start of race.

PRE-TRAINING WARM-UP: Due to medical studies, Sime's time for training is limited. Usually he merely "jogs" 440 yards in 62 seconds, followed by a few stretching exercises, and 330 yards "jog" in 45.0 seconds.

TRAINING: As a high school boy, Dave ran only after baseball practice in baseball uniform. He was a member of a championship high school football and basketball team. As a freshman at Duke University, Durham, North Carolina (1954-55), Dave's primary sports interest was in becoming a professional baseball player, and he trained only after Fall baseball practice. He has been offered $50,000.00 and $60,000.00 by several professional teams to sign a baseball contract. When he ran a 9.8 century in baseball uniform, Duke University head track coach R.L. Chambers recognized him as a "comer." Dave played mostly baseball during his first year at Duke, but ran a few sprint races in respectable but not outstanding times when these races did not conflict with the baseball schedule. In his second year at Duke (1955-56), Sime set the world on fire with his amazing performances in 100 yards, 200 meters, and 220 yards low hurdles. He was in perfect condition, and devoted all his athletic efforts to running. But he overworked by the time the major meetings came around, and this proved his downfall. He was never injured previously, and was accustomed to doing fantastic amounts of work. His training sometimes included 30 hard sprint starts in one workout. This was mostly due to inexperience. Coach Chambers would try to slow him down or get him to rest, but Dave would sneak away and run elsewhere. During his third year at Duke (1956-57), and his fourth year (1957-58), Dave played baseball in the Spring, and participated in track when the baseball schedule did not interfere. He broad jumped in excess of 23 feet, threw the discus 152 feet, and the javelin 210'7", in addition to sprinting. During an AAU trip abroad, he won all of his 24 races during the tour.

SEPTEMBER, 1958 TO JUNE, 1959, due to limited time for training caused by a heavy medical school schedule, Dave could not train as much as he preferred, so he attempted to supplement his running with a weight training program. According to Duke University assistant coach Al Buehler, this proved to be a "mistake." By using small 10 to 30 lbs. dumbbells and leg spats, Dave was able to increase his leg strength to a "tremendous point." He added one inch to the circumference of his thighs and strengthened a groin muscle which he pulled in 1956 to the extent that he could lift 30 lbs. leg spats and perform snappy exercises with these weights. He also used "iron boots" with attached weights. But these exercises did not put his legs into "running condition." The legs were strong and he could now run without fear of pulling a muscle, but running was difficult or without speed. His legs ached much of the time. It took him an abnormally long time to get warmed-up, and feeling good during workouts. Actually he had a miserable time all year, and running was not much fun for him. He managed to win the 100 yards in the Sugar Bowl meeting in New Orleans against little opposition, and ran a 9.4 100 yards at the West Texas Relays where Bobby Morrow defeated him narrowly after Dave got off to a poor start. In Norfolk, Virginia he ran the 100 and 200 meters against the British and French champions, but his times were poor and he felt physically "like an old man." He entered local meetings, but finally gave up when his legs refused to respond to training.

Sime did not race from May, 1959 to September, 1959. During the Summer of 1959 he worked as a counselor at a boy's camp in Michigan, where he ran only occasionally in the woods. Starting in September, 1959 his training was scheduled to consist of daily "overdistance running" with a minimum of work on starting and sprinting. He and his coaches planned to progress slowly with the speed of his training, and as he improved he was to run faster. But Sime is the kind of lad who never wants to operate at half speed, and has consistently run most of his workouts much too fast to suit his coaches. He has been training at noon or at 3:00 PM daily since September, 1959, and his workouts usually last 60 minutes. His weight training now consists of presses up to 180 lbs., jump squats, dips, and chins, with some running up the steps of the Duke University stadium. His running intervals are usually no longer than 440 yards, and he includes numerous 220, 275, and 330 yards repetitions in his training program. His 220 yards repetitions are sometimes faster than 22 seconds on a "good day." However, his workout times (marks) mean little, inasmuch as he often runs in the third or fourth lane because of wet spots on the track, and he frequently finishes short of or beyond the finishing line of his training distances. Dave usually knows what pace he wants to run, and the number or repetitions in any particular workout depend upon the distance, weather conditions, and personal inclination. His recovery between repetitions is not timed or measured, and his coaches prefer that he walk until 80 to 90% recovered before beginning the next running effort. However, due to his limited training time available, he cuts his recovery time to the minimum between repetitions in some workouts. In addition to running, he often sprints over low hurdles for variety. Usually his workouts during winter or pre-competitive season were one of the following: (1) 440, 330, 275, 220, 220, 275, 330, and finally 440 yards. This is Dave's most difficult workout, and he uses it normally on Monday or any day immediately following a day of rest. (2) 6-8x220 yards. Then 4x100 yards fast striding on grass. (3) 2x275 yards. 2x330 yards. 2x220 yards. Very little recovery is permitted between repetitions during this workout, and these repetitions are usually completed within 20 minutes. (4) 6-10x30-40 yards sprint starts with gun. This workout is reserved for warm weather. (5) Weight training indoors, plus calisthenics. This workout is reserved for bad weather. (6) 6-10x10x100 yards easy striding on grass. Then easy starts on grass, according to inclination. This is regarded as a "recovery" type workout. The speed of the above repetitions progress from early season to the start of the competitive season generally as follows: 440 yards (62 to 52 seconds), 330 yards (45 to 39 seconds), 275 yards (37 to 33 seconds), 220 yards (28 to 23.5 seconds, and sometimes 22 seconds or faster.)

COMPETITIVE SEASON: Dave rests one or two days prior to racing. His workouts remain essentially the same, although he concentrates more on starts. His running workouts are faster, more intensive, but the number of repetitions is reduced. Sprint start work receives as much as 75% of the attention during training during competitive season. He participates in two or three indoor meets and approximately 12 outdoor meets annually. Dave still experiments considerably with his sprint start, and is willing to try anything if it seems reasonable. Now he has adopted a consistent rather than a great start such as employed by Ira Murchison. The width of his hands in the "set" position are about shoulder width. He places his front starting block 16 inches behind the starting line, and the rear block 12 inches behind the front starting block. In the "set" position of his start, Sime's hips are approximately level with the shoulders. The weight in this position is somewhat evenly distributed between hands and legs, with slightly more weight on the front foot.

Dave Sime has been plagued by injuries much of his illustrious career, and his failure to gain selection for the U.S. Olympic team in 1956 was apparently due to this reason. Now, in what appears to be his final season in athletics, he has been selected as a member of the U.S. team in the coming Rome Olympics.

Sime won the 1960 Olympic silver medal in the 100 meters in Rome with a 10.2 clocking (same time as gold medal winner Armin Hary).

Dave
Sime

John Smith

JOHN SMITH, Los Angeles Striders and UCLA. Age 22, 1972.

BEST MARKS: Mile, 4:48; 880y, 2:01; 660y, 1:17.4; 440y, 44.5 (world record); 400m., 44.2; 330y, 32.2; 300m., 32.1; 220y, 20.6; 100y, 9.4.

PERSONAL STATISTICS: Born August 5, 1950 at Los Angeles, California. 6'2", 185 lbs. Started racing in 1965 at age 15.

PRE-RACE AND PRE-TRAINING WARM-UP: Jog one mile. 15 minutes calisthenics. Jog an additional mile. 4-6x60-80y sprints. Walk an equal distance after each. Rest five minutes before racing or training.

TRAINING: Smith's training from October through July is essentially the same, differing only in speed as the season progresses. Monday: (a) 550y. Start at 75 seconds in October and gradually reduce the time to 63 seconds in May. (b) 440y. Start at 60 seconds in October and gradually reduce the time to 48 seconds in May. (c) 330y. Start at 45 seconds in October and gradually reduce the time to 35.0 seconds in May. Walk as long as desired for recovery after each. Tuesday and Thursday: Sprints up a 508y grass-covered hill. Start with one in October and increase to five such sprints in January. Walk return recovery after each. After January add 8x110y fast striding, jogging 110y after each. Wednesday: 3x330y. Start at 45 seconds in October and gradually reduce the time to 32-34 seconds in June. Walk as long as desired for recovery after each. Thursday: After the competitive season starts in late February, the Thursday workout changes from repeating Tuesday's training to 3x165y in 15-16 seconds, starting on the curve of the track, followed by 3x150y in 13-14 seconds each. Walk according to inclination for recovery after each. Friday: 5-6x150y. Start at 15 seconds in October, and gradually reduce the time to 13 seconds in May. Once or twice monthly, the Friday workout is changed to 4x220y, starting with 24, 23, 22, and 21 seconds (with running start) in February, gradually reducing the time to 22, 21, 20 plus and 20 plus seconds in May. Walk according to inclination for recovery after each. Saturday and Sunday: Rest. During competitive season, race on Saturday and rest Friday and Sunday.

Smith lifts weights four times weekly, using 3-4 repetitions of the bench press (225 lbs.), curl (95-100 lbs.), and military press (140 lbs.). He jogs 880y warm-down after each workout. Smith attempts to run even pace in competition. When he established his 440y world record, he ran the first half in 22.2 and the final 220y in 22.3. Smith races about twenty times annually, and is coached by Jim Bush. He was ranked first in the world in 1971, recording three of the four fastest times in the world that year. In 1972, he suffered a case of hepatitis early in the year. Yet he still had a 44.3 400m. (second place in the Olympic trials) and was a strong choice for the gold medal in Munich. A leg injury however struck in a pre-Olympic 200m. race and Smith was unable to finish the final 400-meter race at the Games.

John Smith

John Treloar

JOHN FRANCIS TRELOAR, Northern Suburbs AC, Australia. Age 24 years, 1952.

BEST MARKS: 220y, 20.9 (1 ft. downhill course); 110y, 9.5 (following wind).

PERSONAL STATISTICS: 6'3", 184 lbs.

TRAINING: Treloar trains 5 days a week. His pre-competitive training season is divided into 3 parts, each 6 weeks in length. First 6 weeks: Trotting, arm, leg, body exercises, deep breathing. Second 6 weeks: Wind sprints, long run throughs—300 yards, taper off with some stretching exercises. Concentration is on relaxation and correct running posture. Third 6 weeks: Starting, short sharp bursts, few exercises, 220 yards, 150y run throughs—competition.

The duration of workouts is 2 hours starting between 5 and 7 PM. John Treloar has been Australian and British Empire 100y and 220y champion many times throughout his career. Holder of Australian 100 yards record (9.6) which he has run 12 times. Represented Australia in Olympic Games in 1948 and 1952. He reached the 100m. final in 1952, placing sixth.

Ulis Williams

ULIS WILLIAMS, Southern California Striders, Arizona State University. Age 22 years, 1963.

BEST MARKS: 880y, 1:51.0; 440y, 45.3; 220y, 21.0; 100y, 9.8; AAU champion 1962 and 1963.

PERSONAL STATISTICS: Born October 24, 1941 at Hollandale, Mississippi. 6'1", 160 lbs. Started track in 1958.

PRE-RACE WARM-UP: jog 880 yards, stretching exercises, push-ups, sit-ups, hurdle exercise, sprints. Total time 45 minutes.·

PRE-TRAINING WARM-UP: Similar to pre-race.

SUMMER TRAINING PROGRAM: Monday: 2x660 (84-85). Tuesday: 4x330. Wednesday: 8x220 (23.5-24.0); Thursday: 10x110 (11.3), 110 walk interval. Friday: Rest. Saturday: Meet. Sunday: Rest.

WINTER TRAINING PROGRAM: November, 2 mile cross-country. December, 4x440 :54. January, 8x220 (24.0-25.0).

Williams' favorite event is the 400m. which he plans to run in Tokyo Olympics. He considers his 46.1 high school record as his greatest accomplishment. He was ranked first in the world in '62 and '63.

Injured early in the Olympic year, Williams still managed to place fifth at Tokyo. His 45.0 for 400 meters in the Olympic Trials was his best for that distance.

Ulis
Williams

Ross Wilson

ROSS WILSON, University of Queensland Athletic Club, Australia. Age 19, 1969.

BEST MARKS: 400m., 47.3; 200m., 21.1; 100m., 10.5

PERSONAL STATISTICS: Born October 31, 1950 at Brisbane, Australia. 6'4", 175 lbs. He began racing at age 14.

COMPETITIVE WARM-UP: Wilson begins 45 minutes before the actual race. He jogs and walks gradually increasing the tempo. This is followed by light exercises. He places a great deal of emphasis upon the Achilles tendons because of prior trouble. Strides through and starts are then executed.

TRAINING WARM-UP: Exercises and two fairly fast laps are the basics of Wilson's warm-up. He also uses his first few repetitions as part of his warm-up due to the lateness in the evening of his workouts. Wilson does not stretch his hamstrings very much as he feels it may remove some muscle tone.

WINTER TRAINING: Circuit training is a major portion of his winter training program. His final workout this winter (1968) consisted of three rounds of 20 sit-ups, clean and presses (85 lbs.), 20xquarter squats (130 lbs.), 40 straddle jumps (15 lb. dumbbells), 15 bench presses (85 lbs.), 10 curls (85 lbs.), 15 step-ups (85 lbs.), and maximum chin-ups. Most of the winter track work consist of 220 yard repetitions for conditioning. Example workouts include, 40x220 (:29); 8x220 (:26); 6x220 (:25), and 6x220 (:24). He may throw in an occasional 330 workout of 6x330 in 40 to 41 seconds.

COMPETITIVE SEASON WORKOUTS: Sunday: 15-20x50 yards. Tuesday: 4x220 (:25) with 3 minute interval. Wednesday: 6x100 yards with 3 minutes interval. Thursday: 6x150 (:15) with 3 minute interval. Saturday: Competition on inter-squad basis.

Wilson is coached by Les Grove. His main objective in training is the Australian Championships.

Ross Wilson's 45.6 for second place at the Commonwealth Games in 1970 was one of the sensations of the Games.

Hurdling

Lee Calhoun

Lee Calhoun

LEE QUENCY CALHOUN, Roosevelt High School (Gary, Indiana), and North Carolina College.

BEST MARKS: 120 yard HH, 13.5; 110m. HH, 13.2 (established August 21, 1960 at Berne, Switzerland, and equals world-record); 50 yards HH, 6.0; 60 yards HH, 7.1; 70 yards HH, 8.2; 220 yards LH, 22.9; 100 yards, 9.6; 220 yards, 20.9; 300 yards, 30.8; 330 yards, 33.5; 440 yards, 47.0; High Jump, 6'3" (1.905m.); Javelin, 180' (54.86m.); Broad Jump, 22'5" (6.83m.); Shot, 45' (13.72m.)

PERSONAL STATISTICS: Born February 23, 1933 at Laurel, Mississippi. 6'1", 160 lbs. Started racing in 1950 at age 17. Retired from competition in 1960 at age 27.

PRE-TRAINING WARM-UP: (a) Jog 880 yards. (b) 30 side-straddle hops. (c) 30 side bends. (d) With arms straight, swing them both simultaneously 30 times in wide, vertical circles, brushing close to the ears at the top of each circle. (e) Hold arms straight and horizontal with hands in front and palms touching. Swing them horizontally behind back until hands touch. Repeat 30 times. (f) 30 times bending alternately forward and back from waist with hands on hips. (g) 15 times touching elbows to ground while standing with legs spread far apart. (j) Stand with legs spread wide apart. Bend forward with knees straight. Touch ground between legs as far as possible. Repeat 30 times. (k) Lie on back, elevate legs and hips with body weight on shoulders, support hips with hands while elbows rest on ground, and do 30 bicycle or running steps in the air. (l) Leg scissors movements. Lie on ground with weight on shoulders as in (k). Alternately touch the ground behind shoulders with one foot at a time. Repeat 30 times. (m) Lie on ground with weight on shoulders as in (k). Alternately spread legs wide and return, keeping knees straight. Repeat 30 times. (n) 15 sit-ups. (o) 15 leg lifts. (p) Lie on back. Hold legs 6" off ground with knees straight. Spread legs wide and return. Repeat 15 times. (q) Russian dance. Sit in squat position on heels. Jump upward, throw legs out horizontally and return to same squat position. Repeat 10 times. (r) 2x120 yards HH in about 16 seconds. Walk 120 yards after each. (s) Run past the right side of 5 HH at competitive speed and snap the trail (left) leg over each hurdle. Walk back. 8 repetitions. (t) 5x5 HH, concentrating on body lean at take-off, snapping down lead leg after crossing the hurdle, and pull-through of trail leg. Use 5 steps between hurdles. Walk back after each.

PRE-COMPETITIVE WARM-UP: Same as pre-training warm-up, but delete (t), and add 3 times start from blocks and over first hurdle. Then 2x5 HH at full speed. Then lie down for 5-10 minutes with feet elevated. 5 minutes before actual race, walk and jog alternately and perform more stretching calisthenics according to inclination.

PRE-COMPETITIVE SEASON TRAINING: Each workout is preceded by the above described one-hour warm-up. Monday: 4x220 yards in 25 seconds. Walk 220 after each. Tuesday: 10x60 yards in 6.6. Walk 3 minutes between. 5 x gun start from blocks and over first two hurdles plus 10 yards. Walk 2-3 minutes after each. Wednesday: 8x4 HH plus 15 yards at full speed. Walk back to starting line after each. 300 yards in 32-33 seconds. Thursday: 10 x gun start from blocks and over first two high hurdles plus 10 yards. Walk back to starting line after each. 440 yards in 53. Friday: 5x120 yard HH in 14.1. Walk 3 minutes between. Saturday and Sunday: Rest.

COMPETITIVE SEASON TRAINING IN 1960: Identical to pre-competitive training, except Friday's training is eliminated and replaced by complete rest, prior to competition on Saturday.

The above workouts require 2 hours each, usually starting at 3:00 PM. His competitive season usually extended from January through June. He rested July, August, and September and began pre-competitive training in October each year. He never trained more than once daily, and rested only one day prior to competition. His last meal was 4-5 hours prior to racing.

Calhoun did no cross-country racing or weight training, and participated in approximately 12 indoor and 18 outdoor meetings annually. He used a right lead leg over the hurdle. In the starting position, his front (left) starting block was 14″ and the rear (right) block was 24″ behind the starting line respectively. He was coached by Louis Mallard, Dr. Leroy Walker, and Ted Haydon.

The titles won by this great champion are too numerous to mention, but it is significant to note that he won the 1956 and 1960 Olympic 110m. hurdles crowns. He is now assistant track coach at Yale University.

(By Don Kavadas, track coach of Strathmore Union High School, Strathmore, California.)

Rex Cawley

WARREN JAY CAWLEY, University of Southern California. Age 26, 1966.

BEST MARKS: 100 yards, 9.6; 220 yards, 21.2; 440 yards, 46.0; 660 yards, 1:18.0; 120 HH., 13.9; 220 LH., 22.5; 2 miles, 10:15 (at age 18); Broad Jump, 23′6″; High Jump, 6′2″; Discus, 125′; Javelin, 165′; 440yH, 49.6AR, 400mH, 49.1 WR.

Rex Cawley

PERSONAL STATISTICS: Born June 6, 1940 at Detroit, Michigan. 6'0", 160 lbs. Started racing in 1957 at age 16.

WARM-UP: (Both for training and competition). Jog 880 yards. Stretch for 15 minutes. 4x110 yards wind sprints. 3 or 4 practice hurdles. Then 10 to 20 minutes rest before competition.

PRE-COMPETITIVE TRAINING (November 1 through March 15): Monday: 4x440 yards in 60 seconds, 440 jog interval. Tuesday: 660 yards in 1:20 seconds, 550 yards in 1:08 seconds, 440 yards 53-54 seconds. As much interval as needed to recover. Wednesday: 4x330 yards at 37-40 seconds, 440 jog interval. Thursday: 10x160 yards, accelerate to full speed on straightaway, emphasizing high knee lift. Friday: Normal warm-up, then play around with high jump, broad jump, discus, and javelin. Saturday: Rest. Sunday: Rest.

COMPETITIVE SEASON (March 15 through June 1): Monday: 2x550 yards in 1:07-1:08. 440 walk and jog interval. Tuesday: 3x330 yards, 33-35 seconds. 440 walk and jog interval. Wednesday: 3x220 yards, running over 4-36" hurdles, trying for speed plus good form. Interval-walk across infield and start again. Thursday: 3x220 yards, 22-24 seconds. 440 walk and jog interval. Friday: Rest. Saturday: Competition. Sunday: Rest or jog a little if sore or tight (especially in early season).

Rex rarely works out twice a day unless an injury has slowed him before a big meet. Then he will do speed work in the morning and over-distance in the afternoon (usually 550's). His track schedule includes 4 or 5 meets during the indoor season, and competition every weekend during the spring. He has no definite racing tactics, only to win. When not competing on International tours, he rests about 4 months between the competitive season and the beginning of Fall training. His front block is 11" from the starting line and his rear block is 33" from the line. Rex leads with his right leg when hurdling.

Rex won the 1964 400IH title with 49.6, after setting a world record of 49.1 at the US Olympic trials. He was ranked first globally in 1963 and 1964. His American record of 49.6 in the 440IH in 1963 came an hour after a 46.1 quarter mile.

Glenn Davis

GLENN A. DAVIS, Barberton, Ohio High School, and Ohio State University. Age 28, 1962.

BEST MARKS: 440 yards hurdles, 49.9; 400 meters hurdles, 49.2 (world record); 440 yards, 45.7 (world record); 400 meters, 45.5; 220 yards low hurdles, 22.7; 200 meters hurdles turn, 22.5; 200 meters turn, 21.0; 120 yards high hurdles, 14.3; 100 meters, 10.3; 100 yards, 9.6 seconds; broad jump, 24'¼".

PERSONAL STATISTICS: Born September 12, 1934 at Wellsburg, West Virginia. 6', 160 lbs. Started racing in 1951 at age 15. Retired following the 1960 Olympic Games.

WARM-UP: (Identical for race or workout). Jog 880 yards. 10 minutes calisthenics. 6-8x40-120 yards fast striding. Walk an equal distance after each.

TRAINING: Davis did not run cross-country in the fall of the year. He begins training each year in January, starting with two weeks of light jogging daily, gradually progressing the jogging distances. Thereafter he starts the following program which does not change throughout the pre-competitive and competitive season. Most of his workouts are timed. Monday: 10x100 yards in 12 seconds. Walk 100 yards after each. Tuesday: 5x100 yards in 12 seconds. Walk 100 yards after each. 2x300 yards in 33-34 seconds. Walk 440 yards between. Wednesday: Sprint 4-6 times over 300 yards of intermediate hurdles spaced 40 yards apart. Walk 15 minutes after each. Finish with 2x220 yards in 25 seconds. Walk 5-10 minutes between. Thursday: 2x100 yards in 12 seconds. Walk 100 yards after each. 440 yards in 50.5-51.5. Walk 20 minutes. 220 yards in 23-24 seconds. Friday: Rest. Saturday: Competition or time trial. Sunday: Rest.

Davis never trained more than once daily. His workouts ranged from 50 to 120 minutes, beginning at 3:00 PM. He last ate six hours prior to competition. While at Ohio State University he raced annually from March to June or July, as frequently as 50 to 60 times per season, including trials, several events in the same meet, and relay meetings. Another 20 to 40 races per season were added when he participated in summer foreign athletic tours. Thus he was able to remain in top form primarily through much racing. Due to graduation, Davis did not have such intense competition during the 1959-1960 season, although at Rome he nevertheless retained the Olympic 400m. hurdles crown he had won four years earlier at Melbourne.

Davis used 15 steps between the intermediate hurdles, and leads over the hurdles with his left leg. His starting blocks were not kept in the same relative spacing throughout the season, and Glenn did not hesitate to alter his sprint starting position in accordance with personal inclination at the moment.

He was coached by Larry Snyder, who was also 1960 U.S. Olympic Coach. Davis has served as track coach at Cornell and is now in private business.

His versatility as an athlete gives rise to interesting speculation as to what he might have accomplished had he turned his efforts to the decathlon. He has won numerous National Collegiate, National AAU, and Big Ten titles, and the 1956 and 1960 Olympic 400m. hurdles titles.

Davis did not engage in weight training. With respect to his tactics in 440 yards flat racing, Glenn prefers to "start fast over the first 100 yards, level off and relax for 200 yards, and kick the final 140 yards." He hated to lose and was one of the fiercest competitors in track history. He lost only three intermediates races during his career, one while a beginner, the others when out of condition.

Glenn Davis

Jack Davis

JACK DAVIS, University of Southern California. Age 23 years, 1954.

BEST MARKS: 120y HH, 13.6; 220y LH, 22.6.

PERSONAL STATISTICS: Born September 11, 1931 at Amarillo, Texas. 6'3'',
190 lbs. Started racing in 1945 at age 14.

PRE-RACE WARM-UP: Stretching exercises and wind sprints 1 hour prior to
competition.

WINTER TRAINING: Jog on grass 3 days a week, many stretching exercises.

SUMMER TRAINING: Workouts begin with a warm-up and practice on starts.
Monday: 3x220y hard. Tuesday: 5 sets 70y HH. 3 sets of 120y LH.
1x220y. Wednesday: 5 sets 70y HH. 5 sets LH. 1x220y hard. Thursday: 3
sets 70y HH. 1 set LH. 1x100y hard. Friday: Rest, runabout. Light grass
on Sunday.

In addition to numerous NCAA and AAU hurdle championships, Davis placed
2nd in the 1952 Olympic Games 110m. HH and was co-holder of the Olympic
record 13.7. During the competitive season, he races every week, totaling 16
meets. He spends 3 hours on training sessions. Coached by Victor Trouez (high
school) and Jess Mortensen (college).

Jack Davis

Davis, for the second time, became co-holder of the Olympic 110H. record without winning the title in 1956. He was a close second to Lee Calhoun at Melbourne in 13.5.

Keith Gardner

KEITH ALVIN GARDNER, University of Nebraska, Lincoln. Age 29 years, 1960.

BEST MARKS: 440y, 46.6; 220y, 21.0 (20.4st); 100m., 10.3; 100y, 9.5; 120 HH, 13.8; 60 LH (indoors), 6.7 (former American all-comers record).

PERSONAL STATISTICS: Born September 6, 1931 at Kingston, Jamaica. 5'8½", 140 lbs. Started racing in 1945 at age 14. Stopped active competition in 1960.

TRAINING: Gardner trained nine months a year, five days a week. Started weight training in 1960 and lifted for 40 minutes three times weekly. During the winter his training schedule was: Monday: 10-15x80y with a jog between each. Tuesday: 8 starts with 4-6 over 3HH, 2x220. Wednesday: 6 starts, 2-3 over 5HH, 1-2x330. Thursday: Easy striding and jogging. Friday: Rest.

SPRING TRAINING SCHEDULE: Monday: 10x150y with jog in between. Tuesday: 6 starts over 5HH, 1-2x330 or 440 for time. Wednesday: 6 starts, 2-3 over 7HH, 2x220. Thursday: 4-6x150, baton passing. Friday: Rest.

After only one year of hurdling, Gardner broke into world class competition and won the British Empire high hurdles title. He represented Jamaica in the 1956 Olympic Games but failed to progress beyond the first heat. At Nebraska U., Keith took Big 8 titles indoors and out. In NCAA competition, he managed a third in the 220 along with a second in his specialty. The 1960 Rome Olympics witnessed Gardner's last glory as he placed fifth in the 110m. hurdles and garnered a bronze medal as his West Indies' 1600 meter relay team took third place. Coaches who have helped Keith Gardner are Joe Yancey, Frank Sevigne, and G.C. Foster. Athletes who have assisted him are Harrison Dillard, Jack Davis, Andy Stanfield, and Reggie Pearman.

Al Hall

ALFONZO HALL, San Jose City College, California. Age 18 years, 1971.

BEST MARKS: 400 IH, 56.0; 440 yards, 47.0; 330 yards, 33.0; 220 yards, 21.0; 120 yards HH, 13.6 (HS); 100m., 10.5 (e); 100 yards, 9.7 (e).

PERSONAL STATISTICS: Born June 24, 1953 at Chicago, Illinois. 6'1", 170 lbs. Started racing in 1967 at age 14.

PRE-RACE WARM-UP: Jog 4x440 yards. Run over 3 HH from blocks.

PRE-TRAINING WARM-UP: Jog 4x440 yards. 6x60 yards. Track workouts followed by 880 warm-down.

FALL TRAINING: Monday—3x2 miles. Wednesday, Friday—30 minutes jog. Sunday—15 minutes run. Tues. & Thurs., weight training.

WINTER TRAINING: Monday—4x660 yards. Tuesday—Run over 3 HH from blocks, 8x220 yards in 30 seconds. Wednesday—8x300 yards. Thursday—10x60 yards. HH from blocks, 6x220 yards. Friday—10x110 yards.

SPRING/SUMMER TRAINING: Monday—Run over 4 HH. Tuesday—4x330 yards. Wednesday—Run over 6 HH from blocks, 4x220 yards. Thursday—15x110 yards. Friday—8x100 yards. 880y warm-down each day.

Does weight training. Coached by Bill Pendleton, Art Lyons and Bert Bonanno. Participates 3 times indoors and 25 times outdoors annually. 1971 California state 120 yd. HH champion. His best is 14.0 with the college highs.

Hall's best came down to 13.9 as a freshman at San Jose City College in 1972.

Dave Hemery

DAVID PETER HEMERY, Ruislip, and Boston A.A. Boston, Massachusetts. Age 24 years, 1968.

BEST MARKS: ¾ mile, 3:01t; 1000y, 2:12.6; 660y, 1:17.8t; 600y, 1:09.8; 400m., 44.5r; 100y, 9.7e; 440H, 49.6; 400m., IH, 48.1 WR; 120 HH, 13.7; 60y H, 7.1; 50y H, 6.0; 45y H, 5.6.

PERSONAL STATISTICS: Born July 18, 1944 at Cirencester, England. 6'1½", 160 lbs. Started racing in 1954 at age 9.

PRE-RACE WARM-UP: Hurdler's warm-up consisting of jogging, stretching, and hurdling exercises.

PRE-TRAINING WARM-UP: Same as pre-race warm-up.

FALL CROSS-COUNTRY TRAINING: (Hemery was third man on Boston U.'s cross-country team.) *The following workouts are run entirely on golf course:* Monday—AM (7:00), 4-6 miles of easy jogging. PM (4:00), 4x1 mile with mile jog recovery. Tuesday—AM (7:00), 4-6 miles of easy jogging. PM (4:00), 4x1½ miles, 1½ miles recovery jog; 6x2 minutes running at ¾ effort, 5 minutes recovery. Wednesday—AM (7:00), 4-6 miles of easy jogging, PM (4:00), Hill work; 10x "35 seconds" uphill run, 40y recovery walk, spring downhill (28 seconds). Thursday—AM (7:00), 4-6 miles easy jogging. PM (4:00), 5 miles alternating "burst" and jog, (run at 60 seconds 440 pace for 45 seconds jog 2 minutes between each burst). Friday—AM (7:00), 4-6 miles easy jogging. PM (4:00), 1x1½ miles, 4 miles easy jogging. Saturday: One workout on hills usually at 10 AM; either 6x600y hill or 4x880y hill (Both up ski trails), walk down between. Sunday: Rest.

WINTER TRAINING: (Morning exercises now in place of AM running.) Monday—PM, 3x660 in 1:25, walk until completely recovered. Tuesday—PM, 5x300y, walk until recovered. Wednesday—PM, 6 or 8x220, walk until recovered. Thursday—Light striding if a race week. Friday—Rest. Saturday—Race. Sunday—Rest or travel.
(Note: all winter training was done on an outdoor board track, with frequency depending on the weather situation.)

SPRING/SUMMER TRACK SEASON: (All running on a tartan surface; nothing in the morning during this phase.) Monday: 1x660 in 1:20 or 2x660 in 1:23, complete walk-rest between. Tuesday: 3x7IH, complete walk-rest between. Wednesday: 6x220 over IH, walk between. Thursday: Easy light striding. Friday: Rest completely. Saturday: Race. (Usually over 120HH, 440IH, and mile relay. Sunday: Rest.

Hemery lifted weights his junior year while grounded with a severe muscle pull. But he does not use weight training consistently during regular workouts. He competes in 10 cross-country, 20 indoor, and 20 outdoor meets each year. Morning workouts generally take 45 minutes while evening training assumes 90 minutes. Because of the variable and unpredictable weather at his New England locale much of David's workout schedule is determined by opportunity. David Hemery's coaching has included the following men: Dick Sawyer (Thayer Academy), Fred Housden, and Bill Smith (Boston U.).

Besides his 1968 Olympic victory (400m. IH), Hemery has annexed these other titles: Sophomore season: IC4A indoor 60HH record, (7.1); IC4A outdoor 120HH (1st); NCAA indoor 60HH (2nd); England vs. Russia 120HH, (1st); British Empire Games 120HH, (1st). Junior season: (injured). Senior season: Penn Relays (1st); NCAA 440 IH, (1st); British AAA (1st); IC4A (1st). Ranked first in the world in 1968.

STRATEGY: "Because of the step pattern (switching down from 13 strides to 15 over the later stages of the race) there is only one way I can run successfully. (To complete) 13 steps over the early hurdles I have to go almost full speed. . ."

COMMENT: (by Hemery's Boston U. mentor Bill Smith); "All our other (U.S.) 7.1 indoor men would die at the thought of 4-5 mile cross-country races. There are many others who could run great over this distance (400m.) but either through circumstance or attitude won't go after it like David did." "I got the impression there was nothing else I could teach him, but he was so eager, so polite and so co-operative he finally convinced me I was doing a good job—in fact he was doing me a favor. We were a great team and a happy one. Nothing was too much for David. He never shirked a task and I never once heard him moan, although at times I knew he felt like hurling his training gear into the nearest lake. I have known many great athletes but none so naturally gifted, so well behaved and so grateful."

Dave Hemery

Gerhard Hennige

GERHARD HENNIGE, Cologne Sports Institute, Cologne, West Germany. Age 29 years, 1969.

BEST MARKS: 400m. IH, 49.0; (1965 bests included 100m., 10.6; 200m., 21.6; 400m., 47.6).

PERSONAL STATISTICS: Born September 27, 1940 at Karlsruhe, West Germany. 6'2½", 183 lbs. Started racing in 1959 at age 19.

In 1967 Hennige started planned training. He concentrated on the development of general endurance in the winter, included systematic gymnastics to improve his hip mobility, improved his hurdle rhythm, did hurdling around the curve, and attempted to improve his basic speed. His schedule was as follows:

NOVEMBER-MARCH: Day 1: Cross-country 3-4 miles. Day 2: Indoor training (hurdling exercises, hurdling, circuit training and dumbbell exercises). Day 3: 3-4 miles fartlek. Day 4: Indoor training with emphasis on speed development. Day 5: (In park) 5-7x3 minutes runs (850-900m.) with 2 minutes, jog recovery. 15 minutes uphill work.

MARCH-MAY TRAINING: Day 1: Long easy cross-country run with 10-12x200m. sprints on the way. Day 2: (Track) 2 sets of 10x120m. with 50m. recovery jog. Day 3: 30 minutes endurance run, 10x150m. "sharp" sprints with 50m. jog recovery. Day 4: (Track) 100m., 200m., 300m., 400m., 300m., 200m., 100m., in 60-80% effort with 100m. jog recoveries, 10x120m. with 50m. jog recovery. Each track workout, weather permitting, included 20 minutes of hurdle training which consisted of 3x21 laps on the turf surface with 3 hurdles, 15m. apart, on each straight. Occasionally the hurdles were placed on the curve.

MAY-JULY TRAINING: Day 1: 30-40 minutes slow running to recover from Sunday's competition. Day 2: Warm-up with hurdles gymnastics, 5x120m. co-ordination runs, 15 minutes sprint training (starts, short sprints over 30-70m.), 5x150m. wind-sprints, 100m. (11.), 200m., (22.5) 300m., (36.0), 200m., 100m., 10 minutes hurdles (5-10x3-4 hurdles), 10 minutes warm-down. Day 3: 15 minutes warm-up and gymnastics, 8-10 skipping-rope runs over 60-80m. 5x100m. from flying start (10.0) with walk back recovery, 4x200m. (21.5-22.0), with walk back recovery, 3x300m. (35.0-36.0) with walk back recovery. Day 4: 20 minutes warm-up, 15 minutes hurdles gymnastics, 10 minutes hurdle technique work, 3x1HH, 3x3HH, 1x200m. IH, (24.0), 10x120m. on grass. Every 14 days this session concluded with a 300m. IH in 36.5-37.0 seconds. Day 5: 20 minutes hurdle gymnastics and warm-up, 20 minutes light hurdling on grass, 10 minutes warming-down. Day 6: 30 minutes warm-up and gymnastics. Day 7: Competition.

AUGUST-SEPTEMBER TRAINING: Training after the German championships consisted of holding the form by three weekly workouts which concentrated on hurdles rhythm. Emphasis was placed on covering each hurdle distance in 4.0 seconds in the first 200m. and 4.2-4.4 the last 200m. Time trials over 200 and 300m. IH were conducted regularly and the seventh and eighth hurdles were given special attention.

Hennige's training included weights when used with the circuit training program. Coached by Ulrich Jonath, he is primarily known for his performance at the 1968 Mexico Olympic Games where he placed second in 49.0 to David Hemery's world record in the 400m. IH final.

Using the same step-plan as winner Hemery, Gerhard ran the first 6 barriers with 13 strides each, on reaching the 6-7 hurdle interval, he stepped down to a 15 stride rhythm.

Gary Knoke

GARY KNOKE, Oregon Track Club, Randwick Botany Harriers, Australia. Age 27, 1969.

BEST MARKS: 1500m., 4:05; 800m., 1:50.8; 400m., 46.7; 400m. IH, 49.6; 200m., 21.6; 110m. hurdles, 14.0; 100m., 10.7. Placed 4th in 1964 Tokyo Olympics in 400m. h., (50.4). Australian National record 400m. hurdles, (49.6).

PERSONAL STATISTICS: Born February 5, 1942 at Sydney, Australia. 6'4", 176 lbs.

PRE-RACE WARM-UP: Insures looseness and flexibility before starts, run-throughs, and hurdling. Calisthenics used in pre-training warm-up.

PRE-TRAINING WARM-UP: Two to four laps of jogging. Calisthenics (head rolls, trunk twists, forward bends, trunk circles, four to six 100y run-throughs, six to eight starts.

WINTER TRAINING: Knoke runs cross-country three days per week (5-8 miles). Circuit training two days per week. One day hurdling technique.

PRE-SEASON TRAINING: Tuesday and Thursday warm-up, starts, and short hurdling work on speed (8x220). Monday-Wednesday: warm-up, weight training, and warm-down. Friday-Saturday: rest. Sunday: 10 mile cross-country.

minutes). PM, warm-up, 4x440 (first 220 at 27 seconds, second 220 all-out), time around 51-54 seconds depending on time of year, 440 walk between 440's, warm-down. Tuesday—PM, 3 or 4x660 over hurdles (4 hurdles—one every 110 around track; time not important although they should be around 1:30). NOTE: until mid-season flat 660's are run (1:28), warm-down. Wednesday—AM, light jog (2-3 miles). PM, 12x220 (sets of 3—half lap jog rest between sets) first 3 over hurdles at race pace (usually 24-25 seconds), last 9 220's flat out with 4-6 at 27-28; 7-9 at 26-27; 10-12 all-out in 23-24 seconds, warm-down including stadium stairs. Thursday: If competition, work on hurdle technique. Starts and steps to first hurdle, plus between hurdle striding. If no competition, 2x330 hurdles at 38-39 seconds stressing stride and rhythm. Friday: Rest. Light jog (880-1320 to keep loose), light stretching. Saturday: Competition. If not, hard weight workout to maintain acquired strength (on Mondays and Wednesdays until mid-season). Sunday: Rest.

WEIGHT WORKOUT:

Winter weight program:	first of year:	end of year:
1. Squats (on rack)	300 lbs.	450 lbs.
2. Sit ups	100	100
3. Leg lifts*	30	70
4. Hamstring curls	40	120
5. Quad curls*	30	80
6. Toe raises*	150	300

Each exercise with a (*) is done in three sets of ten using only one leg when possible.

*Indoor season weights. The light weight workout consists of only the squats, leg lifts, hamstring curls and quad curls. Total time—approximately 45 minutes. (NOTE: Stretch *after* workout to avoid stiffness).

WARM-DOWN PROCEDURE: Consists of 3 sets of (150 stairs) stadium stairs on Mondays and Wednesdays, other days—880 jog.

Mann, a 14.3 and 19.4 high school hurdler, arrived at B.Y.U. his Freshman year weighing 150 lbs. and towering 6'3¼". Under the tutelage of coach Willard Hirschi, Ralph became the 1969, 1970, and 1971 NCAA champion. His AAU national championship titles in 70 and 71 give further testament to his ever-improving ability. He ranked first in the world in 1971. He ranked fourth in 1970. He was also selected T&FN's 1970 College Athlete of the year. His success, he attributes to both his coach and the integrated training regimen: "I believe that the weight program is what really brought me along as far as strength is concerned; and the distance just got me the endurance I needed."

Competition indoors is limited to 5 occasions, but outdoors he has run as many as 20 times (far too many in his estimation). Mann's 9:00 AM workouts take between 45-60 minutes, his 3:00 PM evening workouts last 120 minutes.

With a left leg lead, he uses a 22-stride approach. In the highs, he sprints 8 strides before take-off. Using a medium-spaced starting position, Mann sets his front block 1'4" from the starting line. His back block is set another 13" to the rear.

STRATEGY: The first six hurdles are negotiated with a 13-stride step plan. On landing after IH No. 6, he switches down to 15 strides. Concentrating on relaxation, Mann tries to come through the 220 in approximately 23.5. On switching down, he focuses his effort on good hurdle form.

Ralph Mann's high school coach was Gerald MacDonald.

In 1972, Ralph Mann set an American record of 48.4 in the 400m. hurdles at the Olympic Trials. In the Munich final his 48.5 was good for second behind John Akii-Bua's record 47.8.

Ralph
Mann

Salvatore Morale

SALVATORE MORALE, Italy.

BEST MARKS: 800m., 1:52.4; 400m., 47.6; 400m., IH, 49.2; 110m. HH, 14.2.

PERSONAL STATISTICS: Born in 1938 at Padova, Italy. 6', 165 lbs. Started racing in 1955 at age 17.

SPRING/SUMMER TRAINING (4 workouts per week): 8x200m. in 27-28 seconds, jog 200m.; specific hurdle exercises. 1x250m. in 32 seconds, rest 6-8 minutes; 2x500m. in 1:15, rest 8 minutes; 1x250m. in 32 seconds. 2x70m. in 6.8-6.9 seconds, rest 70-80 seconds; 2x250m. in 32 seconds, rest 6-8 minutes; 2x70m. in 6.8-6.9 seconds. Specific training over 2-5 hurdles. 3x600m. in 1:35, rest 8:00. 2x500m. last 200m. over hurdles.

WINTER TRAINING (4 workouts per week): 10x200m. in 32 seconds, rest 1:30-2:00. 30x100m. in 15 seconds, rest 1:00-1:30. One hour run on grass. (10 minutes easy run; 100m. in 14 seconds; easy running; 200m. in 30 seconds; easy run; 300m. in 47 seconds; easy run; 400m. in 65 seconds; easy run; 500m.; 10 minutes easy run. Repeat backwards from 500m.-100m.) In the 400m. intermediate hurdles, while leading with his left leg, Morale takes 22 strides to the 1st hurdle and 15 strides between remaining hurdles.

Lubomir Nadenicek

LUBOMIR NADENICEK, Club: TZ Trinec, Trinec, Czechoslovakia. Age 25 years, 1972.

BEST MARKS: 110m. HH, 13.4; 100m., 10.9; also a high jump of 200cm (6'8½").

PERSONAL STATISTICS: Born March 11, 1947. 5'9", 139 lbs. Started racing in 1964 at age 17.

PRE-RACE WARM-UP: 400m.-800m. Gymnastics 45 minutes. 2x100m. in 13 seconds each. 2x1 hurdle. Then 20 minutes before race 1x5 hurdles.

PRE-TRAINING WARM-UP: same as pre-race warm-up.

TRAINING: No fall cross-country training is done.

WINTER TRAINING: Monday: 10 minutes jog. 15 minutes weight lifting (hurdle stretch, leg and crotch extension, trunk flexion). 10x20m. with one hurdle, crouch start at maximum speed each. 20 minutes technique with one hurdle. Jumping half-squats: 3 sets of 2x110kg., 1 set of 5x100kg. and 10x90 kg. Repetition snatching: 3x90kg. 2x100kg. 4x110kg. Abdominal raises: 3 sets of 20x25kg. Side bend: 2 sets of 10x25kg. Overhead roll: 3x15kg. Trunk twisting: 13 sets of 40x25kg. Running on spot 2x30 seconds. Calf raises with 60kg. behind neck. Tuesday: 10 minutes jog. 15 minutes exercises. 7-8x150m.-200m. at 19.5-28 seconds each. Half-jumping squats: 2x120kg. 1x150kg. 1x180kg. 1x200kg. 1x225kg. 1x250kg. Squats 3 sets of 3x90kg. Toe bounce: 2 sets of 10x50kg. Sprint uphill 2x60m. Jog 1200m. Wednesday: 10 minutes jog. 3x100m. in 17 seconds each. 10x3 hurdles maximum speed. 30 minutes basketball. Thursday: 10 minutes jog. 30 minutes gymnastics. 6x100m. in 16 seconds each. 2 sets of (with flying start) 20m. in 2 seconds, 40m. in 4 seconds, 60m. in 6.3 seconds, 80m. in 8.8 seconds, 120m. in 14 seconds and 150m. in 18 seconds. Jog 5 minutes. Friday: 10 minutes jog. Calisthenics, 15 minutes. 5x100 in 15 seconds each. 2x300m. in 44 second each. 2x250m. in 33 seconds each. 2x200 in 27.5 seconds each. 5x100m in 15 seconds each. Hack lift-straddle lift: 90kg. 100kg. 120kg. 5x80kg. Snatch from the hang: 3x60kg. 3x80kg. Forward and lateral raise: 2 sets of 10x15kg. Triceps stretch: 10x18kg. Astride jumping: 2 sets of 15x30kg. Barbell curl: 2 sets of 2x40kg. Bent over curl: 10x50kg. Reverse curl 10x45kg. Rowing motion: 10x40kg. Bench press: 3x50kg., 3x60kg. 2x80kg., 90kg., 95kg., 10x50kg. 20 minutes basketball. Saturday: Long jogging 6-8km. 25 minutes stretching (leg and crotch extensions). High bounding. 15 minutes jog. Sunday: Rest.

SPRING/SUMMER TRACK RACING SEASON: Most every running workout is followed by five minutes jog and trunk flexions. Monday—AM, Jog 10 minutes. 5x100m. in 15 seconds each. PM, Jog 10 minutes 3x100m. 15 minutes stretching and extensions. 5x4 HH. 5x3HH. 300m., in 47 seconds 5x40m. (with gun). 5x30m. (with gun). Tuesday—PM, 45 minutes of exercises (front flip, 30 sit-ups—elbow touches ground, trunk flexions, back lift and arch, full leg swing—alternate). Clean lift to shoulders 3x80kg. 2x100kg., 2x110kg., 1x115kg., 1x120kg. Upper leg lift. Trunk laterals Wednesday: Rest. Thursday—PM, 10 minutes jog. 5x100m. Stretch exercises 15 minutes. 5x120m. low hurdles in 15.6 seconds each. Friday—PM 10 minutes jog. Stretch exercises 10 minutes. 3x100m. 1 or 2x150m. in 18 seconds each. 2x1 HH. Saturday—PM, 5 minutes jog. 10 minutes exercises 3x100m. in 15 seconds each. Sunday: Race 110m. hurdles, leg on 400m relay.

Spends one hour in morning and two hours in afternoon training. One foot from front of starting block to starting line, and two feet between blocks. Nadenicek uses 8 strides to first hurdle and takes off 220-230cm. before hurdle, lead leg comes down 160-180cm. beyond hurdle. Left leg is his lead leg. He has hurdled in the Olympics at Mexico City and placed third in the 1971 Helsinki European

Championship. Racing 35 and more times from April to October, he rests two months before beginning fall training. Coaches include Odehnal, Kaspar and Vitula. He finished 7th in the 110m. H at the 1972 Olympic Games in 13.76. In world ranking he was 8th in 1970, 9th in 1971, 8th in 1972.

Gert Potgieter

CORNELIUS GERHARDUS POTGIETER, Pretoria, South Africa. Age 23, 1960.

BEST MARKS: 440-yard intermediate hurdles, 49.3 (World Record); 440 yards, 46.9; 220 yards hurdles, 23.1 (curve); 220 yards, 21.5; 100 yards, 9.7; High Jump, 6'3"; Triple Jump, 49'5"; Pole Vault, 11'6", Discus, 110 feet; Javelin, 155'; Broad Jump, 22'5".

PERSONAL STATISTICS: Born April 16, 1937 at Pietermaritzburg, Natal, South Africa. 5'10", 160 lbs. Started racing in 1951 at age 14.

WARM-UP: Potgieter's warm-up is identical prior to a race or workout, and usually involves a total of 25 to 30 minutes activity. On warm days it may be shortened somewhat, and on cold days it is lengthened to 40-45 minutes. It consists of four phases normally: (a) 2x440 yards of slow jogging. Walk briefly after each. Then 880 yards of slow continuous jogging; (b) 5-8 minutes of light calisthenics; (c) 4-5x150 yards in spike-shoes. Walk 150 yards after each. The first two are run at ½ full speed, and the remaining 150's are run at ¾ full speed; (d) 8-10 minutes of rest before the workout or race.

Prior to 1958 Potgieter did not engage in Winter or Pre-season training. Instead he played regularly at South Africa's National Game, rugby, until the start of competitive track season. "Gert," as he is known to the world of athletics, achieved a high degree of proficiency in RUGBY (he is a first class provincial three quarter), but sustained a broken neck in 1957, after which he made an amazing recovery.

PRE-SEASON TRAINING: Gert usually trains alone, but to see other athletes training nearby is of much encouragement to him. He always does his training runs at top speed for the particular moment, and is seldom timed with a stopwatch during training. The number of repetitions of a particular distance during a workout depends largely upon how he feels. Gert says, "I don't believe in training to a rigid schedule or according to a stopwatch. I don't run much during training, but when I run I always do it as fast as I can—any distance up to 660 yards. In my opinion it is wrong to let a 440 yards hurdler do 6x660 yards, or 4x660 yards in 90 or 95 seconds. I feel 2x660 yards under 80 seconds are more beneficial. Some of my fellow-athletes do 10x440 yards in 60 seconds each. I do 2x440 yards in below 50 seconds each, and I feel that it is sufficient. I concentrate on less running with more speed." Monday: 2x660y. Walk for full recovery between. Or, three miles of cross-country run over a hilly course. Wednesday: 6-10x150y sprints from starting blocks. Walk an equal distance after each. Thursday: 3x(start from starting blocks and sprint over first three hurdles of 440y. hurdle race—126y total distance each). Then 2-3x330y. Walk for complete recovery after each run. Saturday: Time trials. Usually 2x440y in 52 seconds each. Walk 30 minutes between. Tuesday, Friday, and Sunday: Rest.

TYPICAL TRAINING DURING MIDDLE PART OF COMPETITIVE SEASON: Monday: 2x660y. Walk for full recovery between. Or, three miles of cross-country running over a hilly course. Tuesday: 4-6x150y sprints. Walk five minutes after each. Then 10 sprint starts from starting blocks to (and over) the first hurdle of the 440y hurdle race (49½ yards). Wednesday: 2-3x330y or 440y. Walk until slightly less than full recovery after each. Thursday: Hurdling, 2-3x(start from starting blocks and sprint over first 5 to 8 hurdles of 440 yards hurdle race—201½ to 267¾ yards total distance each). Friday and Sunday: Rest. Saturday: Competition. If no competition is available, then time trials of 2x440y, each slightly faster than 50.0 seconds, with 15 minutes of walking between. Or, one 440y hurdle flight in slightly faster than 52 seconds. On some occasions rest is taken both Thursday and Friday prior to competition on Saturday, in which case hurdling work is done on Wednesday.

Of his technique and tactics, Gert states, "I hurdle alternately and recommend that every 440y hurdler practice leading over the hurdle with either leg. I find it very handy and am convinced that it is to every 440y hurdler's benefit. I consider relaxation more important than speed in 440y hurdling. My coach, Josh Sirakis, always shouts 'relax faster.' In my race strategy and tactics seldom help because all of the runners are in their individual lanes. The faster and fitter man wins. I never try to bluff my opponents."

Gert seldom trains more than once daily, although occasionally on Saturdays he puts in a three miles cross-country run in the morning and repeated sprints in the afternoon. He spends approximately one hour on each workout, usually beginning at 4:00 PM. He participates in 10-15 meets each season. Twice per week he engages in the usually prescribed weight training exercises for the upper body, but does no weight training for the legs. After each day's running (described above), he does apparatus work in the gymnasium consisting of parallel bar, horse, rope climbing, and horizontal bar work.

This youthful Pretoria police detective has already established himself as South Africa's greatest ever athlete. Since hitting a barrier in the 1956 Olympic 400 meters hurdles finals at age 18, he has attained 'veteran' status through capturing the 1958 British Empire Games 440y Hurdles title, winning numerous national titles in his native land, and participating with outstanding success in many countries of Europe. After setting a world record of 49.3 for the 440y hurdles in April, 1960, Potgieter suffered a severe automobile injury that ended his career before the Rome Olympics.

Tom Ryall

TOM CHARLES RYALL, Baptist College, Charleston, S.C. Age 21 years, 1971.

BEST MARKS: 660y, 1:20t; 440y, 47.5r; 330y, 35.0t; 100y, 9.8e; 440 IH, 51.8; 120 HH, 13.8.

PERSONAL STATISTICS: Born June 11, 1950 at Orange, New Jersey. 6'5", 205 lbs. Started racing in 1965 at age 15.

PRE-RACE WARM-UP: Stretching exercises including; hurdle stretch, toe-touches, trail leg exercise, lead leg "pops" over hurdles, knee pops, striding 110's, hurdle runs from blocks over 4-6 hurdles.

PRE-TRAINING WARM-UP: "Heavy" calisthenics, toe touching, splits, hurdle exercises, knee pops, striding (Same as Pre-race except more of each exercise.)

FALL CROSS-COUNTRY TRAINING: (Afternoon workouts—3:30 PM). Monday: 1½-2 hours weight workout. Followed by 4-5 miles on the roads. 3-5 miles at night. Tuesday: Regular warm-up, jog, 25-30x20y steep hills. Concentrate on knee lift, 2 minutes rest between. Wednesday: 1½-2 hours weight workout, followed by running gradual hills as well as 5-6 miles distance. Thursday: Regular warm-up, 8x110 at 9/10 speed, walk 110 for recovery or stride 6x220 in ¾ speed, warm-down. 3-4 miles at night. Friday: 1½-2 hours weight workout, LSD (6-7 miles). Saturday: Distance, 5 miles in afternoon. Sunday: Stretching, light running.

WINTER TRAINING: Same schedule as above.

SPRING/SUMMER TRAINING: Monday: Regular warm-up, jog 2 miles, (30 min.) hurdle work out of blocks, 2x660 in 1:25 10 minutes rest between. Tuesday: Regular warm-up, jog 2 miles, 4x550 (sub 70.0 seconds) lap work. Wednesday: Regular warm-up, 30 minutes of starts of HH, Timed HH race (5-6 hurdles) Timed IH 3x220 IH in 25 seconds. Thursday: Warm-up, 30 minutes on hurdles, 2x440 step-down; 440 (52 seconds), 330

(36 seconds) 220 (23..5), 110 all-out. Saturday: Light jogging. Sunday: Rest.

WEIGHT PROGRAM: Bent arm pull-over — 3 sets at 100, 120, 140 lbs. Dumbbell presses; 3 sets at 65 lbs. Swing curls; 50 lbs. Situps, 50 Dips, 3 sets of 10. Stiff arm extensions with bar, 2 sets of 15 each. Leg curls: 2 sets at 70-80 lbs. Leg extensions: 2 sets at 80-90 lbs. Squats: 3 sets of 10 at 135, 225, 275 lbs.

Ryall's evening workouts last 1 hour. He competes in 5-6 indoor and 24-30 races annually. In high school, Tom was the N.J. Group IV State Champion in the HH. He later annexed the S.C. State championships in the highs and intermediates (13.9 and 51.9). With a right leg lead in both races he takes 8 strides to the first HH, and 13-15 steps between hurdles in the longer race. Tom Ryall has been coached by Robert Kasco, Mike Murphy, and Jim Settle.

Eddie Southern

EDWARD SOUTHERN, University of Texas. Age 21, 1959.

BEST MARKS: Mile, 5:00; 880 yards, 2:00; 660 yards, 1:19; 440 yards, 45.8; 300 yards, 29.9; 220 yards, 20.5; 100 yards, 9.4 seconds; 400m. IH, 49.7.

PERSONAL STATISTICS: Born January 4, 1938 at Dallas, Texas. 6'1", 175 lbs. Started racing in 1952 at age 14.

WARM-UP: (Identical for race or workout). Jog one mile in 6-7 minutes, 5-10 minutes calisthenics. 5x100 yards fast striding. Walk equal after each.

WINTER TRAINING: Monday: 5-7x300 yards @ 35.8 seconds. Walk 140 yards after each. Tuesday & Saturday: Weight training consisting of 4-5 standard exercises emphasizing upper body with poundage of 70-125 lbs. Standing and 180-200 lbs. on bench. Then 2-3 sprints up stadium of 67 steps. Walk down. Wednesday: Spring starting practice. Hurdle practice. 7-10x150y @ 17 seconds. Walk 150y recovery after. Thursday: 4-6x440y @ 54 seconds. Walk 440 after. Friday: 2 miles cross-country jogging on golf course. Sunday: Rest.

SPRING TRAINING (April): Monday: 550, 660, or 880y at 60 seconds 440y speed, with sprint at finish. 300y @ 33.5 with sprint finish. 220 @ 23. 100y sprint. Walk equal distance after each. Tuesday: 6-10 short sprint starts from blocks. Walk back. Then 50y, 75y, and 100y sprints from blocks. Walk equal distance after each. Wednesday: 2-3x220 @ 22.5. Walk

5 minutes after each. Thursday: Warm-up *only*. Friday: *Rest or compete.* Saturday: Competition. Sunday: *Rest.*

Duration of workouts: 1½ hours at starting at 3:30 PM.

Participates in approximately 40 races per year including heats. Prefers to run first and last 220 at same pace in 440 race. Coached by Clyde Littlefield. Member 1956 Olympic Team. Earned the silver medal in the 400m. IH.

WEIGHT TRAINING: 2 sets, eight repetitions each of clean and jerk, military press, curl, forearm pull, lateral raises, bench press. Poundage 10 lbs. per hand on lateral raises. 105 lbs. bench press, 70 lbs. all others. Poundage increases and repetitions decrease as season progresses.

Eddie Southern

Spencer Thomas

SPENCER THOMAS III, George Washington Carver Sr. H.S., Opelousas, Louisiana. Age 18 years, 1968.

BEST MARKS: 440y, 49.2; 330 IH, 37.7; 330y, 33.8t; 220y, 21.8t; 120 HH, 13.7n (42"-14.2n); 100m., 10.9t; 100y, 9.7t.

PERSONAL STATISTICS: Born August 18, 1950 at New Orleans, Louisiana. 5'10½", 156 lbs. Started racing in 1963 at age 12.

PRE-RACE WARM-UP: Run ½ mile, walk a 220, finish with 5x50y dashes.

PRE-TRAINING WARM-UP: Same as Pre-race except 4x220 is substituted for 5x50y dashes.

SPRING/SUMMER TRAINING: Monday—PM, (3:30), warm-up, 10 minutes walk, 5x100y dash out of blocks (3 for time), walk 10 minutes, 5x220y dash out of blocks (3 for time). The 100's must be 10.0 or faster, the 220's 22.0 or faster. Tuesday—PM (3:30), warm-up, walk 10 minutes, 3x330y, 4x120y (sub 13.0), walk 10 minutes, jog 1 mile with high knee action, walk 10 minutes. Wednesday—PM, (3:30), warm-up, walk 10 minutes, stride 4x440y, stride 4x150y, 8x40y starts, walk 10 minutes (Spencer finished with LJ technique work). Thursday—Competition. Friday—Light day if race on Saturday, jogging and striding. Saturday—Competition. Sunday—No training.

Spencer Thomas

Thomas lifts weights the first week of training doing "leg and chest work" of 30 reps each. Outdoors he runs a prolific 85 races with football substituting for cross-country and no indoor meets. His evening workouts last from 3:30 to 5:00 PM. The former national record holder in the triple jump (49'5") was named co-captain of the Orlando Sentinel's All-Southern track and field squad. Spencer is also rated in the top 15 of the all-time best high school hurdlers for the college style barrier. With a right leg lead Thomas takes an unusual 9 strides to the first hurdle. His starting blocks are set in a "bunch" style with 3" separating the blocks and a distance of 1 foot between the starting line and the front one. Spencer Thomas has been coached by Lionel Fleury and Enos Hicks.

Jaako Tuominen

AIMO JAAKKO TUOMINEN, H.K.U. Helsinki; B.Y.U., Provo (Utah-USA). Age 25, 1969.

BEST MARKS: 1500 SC, 4:20; 1500m., 4:04.0 (age 16); 1200m., 3:04.0 (t); 1000m., 2:32.0 (age 17); 1000y, 2:14; 880y, 1:50.0; 800m., 1:48.4; 660y, 1:18.1 (t); 600m., 1:17.0 (e); 440y, 48.6; 400m., 46.9; 440y IH, 51.5; 400m. IH, 50.4; 330y, 34.3 (e); 300m., 34.1 (t); 220y, 22.1; 200m., 21.5; 110m. HH, 15.8; 120y HH, 15.0; 100m., 11.0; 100y, 10.0.

PERSONAL STATISTICS: Born May 4, 1944 at Orimattila, Finland. 6'1", 176 lbs. Started racing in 1961 at age 17.

PRE-RACE WARM-UP: 2-3 miles in 30 minutes, including ¾ mile jogging, calisthenics, ½ mile at faster speed, 3 easy 250's on grass and 2x100m. fast striding.

PRE-TRAINING WARM-UP: 3-4 miles in 30 minutes (fartlek) with calisthenics and 3x100m.

FALL CROSS-COUNTRY TRAINING: Monday: 8 miles run. Tuesday: 4 miles run, 6x300m. Wednesday: 6-10 miles long fartlek. Thursday: weight lifting, 6x220. Friday—AM, 4 miles fast run. PM, 6 miles. Saturday: rest. Sunday: 10 miles.

WINTER TRAINING: Monday and Tuesday: 8 miles. Wednesday: weight lifting, 4 miles run, 8x220. Thursday—AM, 4 miles. PM, 3x600. Friday—AM, 4 miles. PM, 6 miles. Saturday: 9 miles, 8x330. Sunday: 8 miles fast fartlek.

SPRING/SUMMER TRAINING: Monday: easy 8 miles. Tuesday: 4 miles, 4x220, 4x330. Wednesday: 4 miles, 9x600 (fast). Thursday: 6x220 (fast).

Friday: long easy run. Saturday: rest. Sunday: long fartlek.

Duration of workouts: morning, 30 minutes starting at 10 AM; evening, 1½ hour starting at 4 PM. Weight training: 3 sets of leg press with 500 lbs. (6 reps). Tuominen rests the day prior to competition. He has a year-around training program with usually 5 indoor races in February- March, 35 outdoor races from March (USA) or from June (Finland) until September; no cross-country races. Tuominen is coached by Rolf Haikhola, Oswald Mildh and Willard Hirschi (USA). He represented his country in two Olympic Games: 1964 and 1968. Finnish champion 1964, '66, '67, '68, '69. Scandinavian champion 1963. Captain of national team 1968-69. As a 400m. hurdler he leads his right leg over the hurdle, uses 22 or 24 strides to the first hurdle and 15 strides between hurdles.

Marcus Walker

MARCUS TYRONE WALKER, University of Colorado, Boulder, Colorado. Age 21,1971.

BEST MARKS: 440y, 46.0; 330y, 44.0; 220y, 20.5; 100y, 9.4; 110m. HH, 13.3; 120y HH, 13.1.

PERSONAL STATISTICS: Born February 10, 1950 at Ft. Smith, Arkansas. 6'2", 178 lbs. Started racing in 1965 at age 15.

PRE-RACE WARM-UP: Jog 1 mile, exercise 30 minutes, hurdle until loose.

PRE-TRAINING WARM-UP: Jog 1 mile, stretch until loose. Workout followed by 880y warm-down.

FALL TRAINING: Monday, Wednesday, and Friday: jog 4½ miles. Tuesday and Thursday: jog 5 miles; practice over 3 hurdles at ½ speed. Saturday: 1 hour of stretching; jog 30 minutes. Sunday: 30 minutes of stretching.

WINTER TRAINING: Monday: 3x220y in 27 seconds; 1x440y in 62 seconds; 1x330y in 42 seconds. Tuesday: Jog 2 miles; hurdle techniques. Wednesday: 3x220y in 30 seconds; 1x440y in 60 seconds, rest 3 minutes; 1x550y in 1:30, rest 4 minutes. Thursday: 15x60 yards. Friday: 15 starts; stretch over hurdles. Saturday: Jog 4 miles; 1 hour stretching. Sunday: Rest.

SPRING/SUMMER TRAINING: Monday: 3x220y in 30 seconds, rest 2 minutes; 3x330y in 45 seconds, rest 3 minutes; 2x440y in 65 seconds, rest 3 minutes. Tuesday: 15x110y; 10x120y HH. Wednesday: 4x220y in 30 seconds, rest 2 minutes; 6x330y in 45 seconds, rest 3 minutes; hurdle stretching. Thursday: 4x220y in 30 seconds, rest 2 minutes; 10x110y; 1x440y in 65 seconds. Friday: Hurdle technique. Saturday: Jog 4 miles. Sunday: Rest.

In Walker's starting position, his front block is 1' behind the starting line and his rear block is 18". In the 120y/110m. hurdles, he leads with his right leg and takes 7 strides to the first hurdle.

Does weight training. Coached by Jack Kinchlae, J.D. Edmonson, Dale Remsberg, and Don Meyers. Competes annually 10 times outdoors and 10 times indoors. Tied world indoor records in 60y dash, 60y low hurdles, and 50y high hurdles. He ranked 2nd in the world in 1970, and competed on the US international team, winning the USA-USSR 110m. hurdles. Injuries have hampered Walker since then.

Marcus Walker

Ron Whitney

RON WHITNEY, Occidental College, California Striders. Age 25, 1967.

BEST MARKS: 880, 1:48.6; 440, 47.1; 440 intermediate hurdles, 49.3.

PERSONAL STATISTICS: Born October 5, 1942 at Modesto, California. 6'1½", 172 lbs. Began racing at the age of 14.

WARM-UP: Jog one mile, 4x100y sprints.

WINTER TRAINING: Monday: 4 sets of 4x220 in :27. Tuesday: 16x110. Wednesday: 2-3x330. Thursday: 4 sets of 4x110. Friday: 4 sets of 4x220 or time trial. Saturday: jog two miles. Sunday: Rest.

SUMMER TRAINING: Monday: 2x330 in 33-34. Tuesday: 3x4x220 over 30" hurdles. Wednesday: 550-330-220. Thursday: Starts over first hurdle. Friday: Rest. Saturday: meet. Sunday: Rest.

Ron does weight work with low poundage and high repetitions. He is coached by Atis Petersons and Chuck Coker.

Ron became one of the world's best intermediate hurdlers in 1967 and 1968. In 1967, he ranked first in the world with a best of 49.3. In 1968, he had a lifetime best of 49.0 and placed sixth in the Olympics, clocking 49.2.

Athletic Weekly, Vol. 21, No. 36, September 9, 1967.

Ron
Whitney

Fred Wilt

NOTES ON SPRINTING

1. Modern day sprinting includes all flat races below 880 yards (800 meters). However, the 440 yards (400m) is an "endurance sprint."

2. 100m equals 100 yards plus 9.36 yards. 200m equals 220 yards less 1.28 yards. 400m equals 440 yards less 2.56 yards.

3. 100 yards (91.44m) time plus 0.9 second equals 100m (109.36 yards) equivalent time.

   220 yards (201.16m) time less 0.1 second equals 200m (218.72 yards) equivalent time.

   440 yards (402.34m) time less 0.3 second equals 400m (437.44 yards) equivalent time.

   220 yards straightaway time plus 0.4 seconds equals equivalent 220 yards time around a turn.

4. A sprinter's 440 yards potential may be approximated by multiplying 2 x his best 220 yards, and adding 3.5 seconds.

5. An "easy sprint" is an absurdity or phenomenon which should never exist, because sprinting means running at the flat-out, absolute maximum speed of which the athlete is capable! However, all sprint races are not run absolutely flat-out. Nevertheless, even the longest sprint today is run only a fraction under full speed. The objective in sprinting is to achieve sheer speed above all else. The standard of sprinting is so high today that even though sprinters may be born and not made, correct technique and proper training are necessary to achieve success. The speed of contraction of a single muscle fiber cannot be changed. This implies speed is inherent. However, the ability to co-ordinate the power of any related muscle groups is an acquired ability. Thus sprinting speed can be improved through proper training.

6. Improvement of sprinting action involves refinement and strengthening of natural running movements. Individual differences in physique, height, muscle leverage, and temperament result in differences in style. Improved form and technique involves discarding wasteful movements, and strengthening and co-ordination of efficient movements.

7. Sprint speed depends upon stride length and rate of striding or cadence. The cadence in good sprinting is 4½ (and sometimes possibly 5) strides per second.

8. Stride length among sprinters varies between about seven feet (82 inches) and 8½ feet (102 inches) or 2.10 to 2.60m. Optimum stride length in sprinting may be approximated by multiplying the runner's height by 1.17, and adding or subtracting 4 inches.

9. Improving either stride length or cadence will increase speed. However, it is useless to improve one at the expense of the other. The rate of striding is governed by individual differences, and for any one individual sprinter there is not great room for improvement of stride cadence. Stride length, therefore, offers the best opportunity for improving sprint speed.

Example:

Stride Length	x Cadence	equals	Horizontal Speed
7 feet	x 5 strides per second	equals	35 feet per second
8 feet	x 4½ strides per second	equals	36 feet per second

10. Due to individual differences, each sprinter has his own most efficient stride length. By developing greater muscular strength, elasticity, and joint mobility, the stride length may be increased naturally. Stride length is increased primarily by thrust of the leg against the ground, acting behind the body's center of gravity. Greater stride length cannot be achieved by placing the forward foot ahead of the body's center of gravity.

11. The sprinter is propelled (driven) forward by the forceful extension of the hip, knee, and ankle joints of the leg in contact with the ground, together with the quick, forceful pull through of the other (recovery) leg. It is the range of movement of the arms and legs while the runner is still in contact with the ground which produces stride length. Understriding entails incomplete extension of the joints of the leg in contact with the ground, and in incomplete pick-up of the knee of the other leg. Overstriding results from reaching forward with the foot of the recovery leg as it approaches the ground, in an effort to place this foot ahead of the body's center of gravity.

12. Within limits, stride length is proportional to running speed. The sprinter does not consciously try to increase his stride length, but rather stride length automatically increase because of the speed at which he runs. The faster the racing speed, the longer the stride. The slower the running speed, the shorter the stride.

13. Technically correct, efficient movements, plus greater muscular strength, combined with correct training, will tend to improve cadence in the unlikely event it is less than the 4½ strides per second used by top class sprinters.

LEG ACTION

14. After the recovery leg leaves the ground following completion of the drive, it begins to flex. As the thigh (upper leg) swings forward the lower leg folds up more and more, thus causing the foot of this leg to rise very high toward the seat. This high "kick-up" of the recovery foot is not a wasteful movement. It is a natural reaction to the thrust of this leg while it was in contact with the ground and the following swing through of the thigh. It also permits the leg to be brought through in the recovery phase as a compact, short lever, thus increasing the speed of movement.

THE DRIVING LEG

15. The body is propelled forward by the extension of the lever at the hip, knee, and ankle, applied when the foot is in a position behind the runner's body weight, pushing him forward. As the foot of the recovery leg moves toward the track in front of the body, it moves downward, apparently backward, to make contact with the ground beneath the body's projected center of gravity. The driving leg should propel the body forward throughout the time the foot is in contact with the ground behind the center of gravity causing the feeling of pushing the ground away from the body.

FOOT ACTION

16. Keep the feet pointing straight ahead. The outer edge of the ball of the foot makes contact with the ground first, immediately followed by the heel resting on the ground momentarily. As the foot touches the ground, the knee is bent. As the body's center of gravity continues forward, the heel is lifted, and forceful extension of the levers at the

hip, knee, and ankle propel the body forward. Except for the first few strides after the start, the heel should touch the track without reservation (uninhibited) with every stride, in a "ball-heel-ball" foot-plant action. Both feet are off the ground about 60% of the time in sprinting.

ARM ACTION

17. Emphasis on arm movement is forward and backward, although there will be a slight turning inwards toward the midline of the body. The hands come slightly across the body, but do not swing farther than the midline of the trunk. The legs set the pace for the arms in sprinting. Right arm and left leg move in co-ordination, and the left arm and right leg move in co-ordination. Arm speed will affect leg speed. Since the arms affect leg speed, with the onset of fatigue they may be used to lead the leg movement. Vigorous arm action helps keep the shoulders square to the front in sprinting. The hands rise up to about eye level in front, and travel no more than a foot behind the hip-line at the rear. The range of arm motion is approximately the same in front as behind the shoulder axis. When the hand is farthest to the rear of the body, the upper arm is almost parallel to the ground. As the arm moves forward from its position to the rear of the body, it decreases the bend at the elbow to less than 90 degrees when the hand is near eye level in front. As the arm moves backward, the angle at the elbow is greatest when the arm is roughly parallel to the trunk, and again decreases when it reaches its farthest point to the rear of the body.

CARRIAGE OF HEAD AND TRUNK

18. The head remains in normal alignment with the trunk. After the start, fix the eyes on the track about 30 yards ahead. In actual competition, sprinters probably don't remember where they focus their eyes.

FORWARD LEAN (BODY ANGLE)

19. Forward lean is dependent upon wind resistance and rate of acceleration. Lean further forward when running into a strong wind to offset the resistance produced by the wind. The reverse effect is evident with a strong tailwind.

20. When the rate of acceleration is at its greatest, the forward lean must be at its greatest. The sprinter has great forward lean at the start of his sprint race. From the moment he starts to the point where he reaches top speed, acceleration gradually diminishes although speed increases. Forward lean gets less and less as top speed is reached. Running in a vacuum at top speed, there would be no lean at all. Body angle (lean) is proportional to acceleration. The greater the acceleration, the more the forward lean. The less the acceleration, the less the forward lean. Body lean is a function of acceleration. No acceleration, no lean!

LINE OF RUNNING

21. Run *in* a straight line, which does not necessarily mean *on* a line. Any movement which draws or pushes the sprinter from one side to the other is wasteful and adversely affects speed. Efficient running means a minimum of wasted energy and a maximum of effort directed to the task of driving the runner forward.

RELAXATION

22. Relaxation is very much a state of mind, and is achieved by practice and more practice at sprinting. Tense only those muscles immediately concerned with forward propulsion. Unnecessary tension means wasted effort. Over-tension makes it difficult to move the arms rapidly through proper range. There are about 43 to 45 strides in a 100 yards race. It requires 46 to 49 strides to sprint 100 meters. The muscle groups involved in each

stride undergo a lightning fast switch from contraction to relaxation. The sprinter's secret is the ability to make this switch skillfully and to maintain a relaxed style of running without decreasing the force of his drive. Relaxation requires skill plus the strength necessary to apply it.

BREATHING

23. Breathing is essential! Let it come naturally. Breathe both in and out of mouth and nose without reservation. Fast running is the best breathing exercise.

BASIC STARTING TECHNIQUE

24. Sprinting is a pushing, not a pulling action. This is especially true at the start of the race. Thus the sprint starting position from a crouch, with body weight well ahead of the feet. The greater the acceleration (as at the start where acceleration is greatest), the more need to pitch the body weight well in advance of the feet. Research has proved the "medium" start best, as reflected in the article entitled "Research on Sprint Running", by Franklin M. Henry, which appears in "The Athletic Journal" (Feb., 1952, Vol. 32, No. 5, page 30).

STARTING BLOCKS

25. In the "medium" start, the front block should be 15 to 18 inches behind the starting line, and the rear block 16 to 20 inches behind the front block. A simple method of determining block placement in the medium start is to place the heel of one foot up to but behind the starting line, with the toes pointing opposite to the direction of the run. Measure three or four inches beyond the toe, and draw a line through this point. Set the front block on this line. Bring the rear knee opposite the toe of the front foot, and place the rear block in accordance with this position.

26. Fix the front block at an angle of 60 degrees. Adjust the rear block to an angle of 85 degrees.

THE "ON YOUR MARKS" POSITION

27. At the command of "on your marks", walk from behind, forward of the blocks. Place the hands on the ground beyond the starting line. Back into the blocks. Insure the toes are in contact with the ground. Arms should be shoulder width apart. Kneel with the rear knee on the ground.

THE "SET" POSITION

28. At the starter's command "set", move the shoulders to a position slightly in front of the starting line. Raise the hips slightly above shoulder level. The front knee is bent at an angle of approximately 90 degrees. The rear knee is bent at an angle greater than 90 degrees, somewhere in the area of 120 degrees, depending upon the individual. The arms are unbent directly below the shoulder joints over bridged fingers directly behind the starting line, so as to keep the shoulders as high as possible. Keep the head in natural alignment with the shoulders and fix the eyes on a spot not more than three feet beyond the starting line. Some sprinters take a deep breath and hold it for the gun. Others regard this as unnecessary. In the "set" position, if a plumb-line were dropped from a line between the shoulders, it would fall one or two inches in front of the starting line.

A novice may get into the "set" position by first moving (not jerking) the shoulders forward, and then raising the hips. With experience, these two movements will merge into one, and the action becomes one of rocking forward-upward into the proper position.

In supporting the sprinter's weight in the "set" position, it should be divided roughly between the arms and front leg, with no weight on the rear leg. The amount of weight supported by the arms will be influenced by the strength of the sprinter's arms. Too much weight supported by weak arms will cause a sprinter to stumble as he drives out of the blocks. There should be sufficient weight on the arms so that if the hands are suddenly snatched from the ground, the trunk will fall forward-downward, not merely downward. The rear foot should be firmly against the back block.

THE "GUN"

29. IAAF Rule 162, para. 5, specifies that on the command "Set" all competitors shall at once and without delay assume their full and final set position. Failure to comply with the command after a reasonable time shall constitute a false start. The sprinter's attention in the "set" position should be concentrated upon the forthcoming sprint motion or action, and *not* upon the sound of the gun. Research studies have proven that in various motor-muscle responses the average reaction time when concentrating on a sound stimulus is 0.225 second, whereas when concentrating on the forthcoming motor response, the reaction lapse is only 0.120 second. This full one-tenth second difference makes obvious the advantage of concentrating attention on the *forthcoming action* while in the "set" position. Concentrate on one definite thought while in the "set" position, such as a fast arm action or fast, high knee lift. The start itself should become an automatic reaction to the gun.

30. IAAF Rule 162, which specifies starting regulations, does not limit the starter to any definite period of time after the command of "set" before he fires the gun. His duty is to insure that all contestants are steady on the mark before the race is started. However, it has been demonstrated that about two seconds is the best interval of time for a fair start. NCAA Rule 19 in the U.S.A., does, however, specify that at the command of "set" all competitors shall at once and without delay assume their full and final set position. "Then, after an interval of approximately two seconds and when all are motionless, he shall discharge the pistol."

31. As the gun is fired, snatch the hands from the track and drive off with both feet against the blocks. Sprinters never lift the rear foot directly forward at the sound of the gun, but thrust with lightning speed against the rear block before moving this foot forward. Pull the back foot through with a powerful and high knee action. There must be fast, powerful counterbalancing arm action to compensate. Drive the body hard and low over the ground. The rear foot is snapped forward to the ground at least 18 inches beyond the starting line. Avoid raising to an upright position too soon by powerful acceleration. Run out of the blocks, don't patter out with short mincing steps. A high fast knee lift is a fundamental of good sprinting from the first to the last stride. One temporary remedy for beginners raising up too quickly into an upright position at the start is to look at the knees the first few strides. Remember, drive out of the blocks with *long, fast strides;* never short fast strides!

THE STARTING STRIDES

32. In good starting, the first stride will be the shortest, the second stride an inch or so longer, and then each succeeding stride will lengthen until full stride length is reached. The first eight or ten strides increase appreciably as the body gradually reaches a more upright position. Each of the first 20 strides or so successively increase in length.

THE RACE

33. The arm action is powerful, regular, vigorous, and fast. This permits the shoulders to remain generally square to the front in the direction of the race. High knee action, powerful long strides, good range of movement of arms and legs, emphasis on the sweep back of the leading leg and arm, feet pointing straight ahead, knees brought through close to one another, relaxation in the hands, arms and shoulders as much as possible

while maintaining a powerful arm action—these are all characteristics of good sprint technique. Maximum speed is reached in about six seconds. Top sprint speed is about 36 feet per second. Top sprinters develop about 14 horsepower running 100 yards.

As the sprinter reaches top speed, he has less and less time in which to apply force (thrust) behind his center of gravity while his foot is in contact with the ground. Perhaps a distinguishing characteristic of a great sprinter is his ability to still apply considerable thrust as he moves faster and faster.

THE FINISH

34. Run through the finish with no gyrations, gymnastics, lifting of arms to breast the tape, etc. If a lunge or dip finish is used, reserve it for the final one or two strides.

220 YARDS and 200 METERS

35. Novice sprinters are usually advised to divide their 220 yards sprint race into the acceleration at the start (about 60 yards), the "float" or "coast" (about 100 yards), and finishing effort (about 60 yards). The float implies reduction of tension involving only an imperceptible reduction of speed, no change of form and retaining speed with the least possible effort. Greater relaxation in the arms, dropping the hands slightly in the backswing, greater relaxation about the hips, thus permitting a greater stretch of the thighs, will help to maintain speed with minimum effort.

36. The day will come when many top class sprinters run 220 yards on the curve under 20.0. When this happens there will be no time to relax into a "float". At that speed, the 220 yards must be run as a single unit, sprinting as fast as possible with minimum tension the entire distance, utilizing a "sprint" tactic of maximum acceleration, minimum deceleration!

REFERENCES

Marlow, Bill, *Sprinting and Relay Racing.* Amateur Athletic Association: London, 1972.

Doherty, Kenneth J., *Track and Field Omnibook.* Tafmop Publishers, Swarthmore, Pa., 1971.

Dyson, Geoffrey H.G., *The Mechanics of Athletics.* University of London Press Ltd.: London, 5th edition, 1970.

Powell, Dr. John T., *Track and Field Fundamentals for Teacher & Coach.* Stipes Publishing Company: Champaign, 1962.

Wilt, Fred, *Run Run Run.* Track and Field News: Los Altos, 1964.

THEORETICAL EXAMPLE OF TRAINING FOR A MATURE 100-220 YARDS SPRINTER

(Note that this is merely a theoretical example used for instructional purposes only and should not be dogmatically applied in actual coaching. Further, this program is not intended for younger or beginning sprinters).

OFF-SEASON TRAINING: Monday, Wednesday, Friday—3 to 5 miles cross-country followed by weight training. Tuesday—4 to 8 x 440 yds. in 70 seconds. Walk until heart

Fred Wilt

REVIEW OF HIGH HURDLE TECHNIQUE

THE STARTING POSITION:

1. Use a sprinter's crouch start with "medium" block spacing. This places the front starting block 15 to 18 inches (38 to 46 centimeters) behind the starting line, with a space of 16 to 20 inches (40 to 50 centimeters) between the front and rear blocks. When "ON-YOUR-MARK", the rear knee should be opposite the toe of the front foot. The front block should be set at a 60 degree angle, and the rear block at an angle of 85 degrees. In the "SET" position the front knee is bent at an angle of about 90 degrees, the rear knee at an angle slightly greater than 90 degrees, the hips are somewhat higher than the shoulders, the body weight is on the hands and front foot, the head is held in natural alignment with the body, and the eyes are focused somewhere between the starting line and two or three feet (60 to 90 centimeters) beyond the starting line.

2. The starting position may be modified somewhat to perfect the approach to the first hurdle. This modification may take the form of slightly increasing or decreasing the distance from the line to the first block, and spacing between blocks.

3. Most hurdlers use eight strides to the first hurdle. In the starting position using the eight stride approach plan, the lead foot is placed on the rear block and the take-off foot is placed on the front block. If a seven stride approach is used, these positions are reversed with the lead foot on the front block and take-off foot on the rear block.

APPROACH TO THE FIRST HURDLE:

4. Perfecting the approach to the first hurdle is accomplished by trial and error. Adjust the approach by lengthening the 4th, 5th and 6th strides. Keep strides one, two, and three, and strides seven and eight normal.

5. Because the take-off for the first barrier is about 13 yards (11.90 meters) from the start, the hurdler must get into the normal sprinting angle and sprinting stride rhythm sooner than the sprinter.

6. Make no effort to look at the first hurdle until after the first three or four strides from the start. Thereafter, fix the eyes on the hurdle rail ahead.

7. The arms function as in sprinting except during hurdle clearance.

8. Try to reach the first hurdle first in competition. This necessitates negotiating the approach as fast as possible. Greater approach speed permits a more horizontal take-off thrust, which results in a lower, flatter, faster hurdle clearance.

9. Slightly shorten the last stride prior to take-off. This rotates the trunk forward so the drive from the take-off foot will project the body with an almost horizontal lean or "body-dip" across the hurdle. Body-dip must start on the ground, as the flight path of the center of gravity (CG) is pre-determined when in the air and cannot be altered while airborne. For

most hurdlers using an eight stride approach, this means the eighth stride is shortened before take-off.

THE TAKE-OFF:

10. The take-off point is a 6½ to 7½ feet (1.98 to 2.29 meters) from the barrier. The take-off distance before the hurdle depends upon speed of approach, height of the athlete, length of leading leg, and effective speed of lead leg action.

11. 90% of effective clearance of the obstacle is determined at take-off. Leave the ground with sufficient body-lean or dip to clear the hurdle with a minimum of upward movement. The body-dip makes it possible to raise the seat and lower the trunk in relation to the center of gravity as the hurdle is crossed.

12. Depart the ground from the ball of the take-off foot with the toes pointing straight ahead.

13. The center of gravity and body weight are ahead of the foot at take-off.

14. Keep hips and shoulders square to the line of running at all times, including take-off.

15. At take-off, lift the lead leg directly forward with the knee well bent, in the line of running, as though executing an exaggerated running stride. Again, the shoulders remain square to the direction of the run.

16. The lead leg at take-off must be lifted fast, with knee well bent. This bent lead knee must of course be lifted higher than in normal sprinting. A high, fast pick-up of the knee of the lead leg encourages continuation of general sprint action, increases force of thrust off the ground by the take-off leg in reaction to the increased force resulting from the fast knee-lift, leaves behind the take-off leg (trail leg) resulting in a good split position after take-off, increases body-dip in reaction to the fast knee-lift, permits getting closer to the hurdle for the take-off than would be possible with a straight lead leg, and is much faster than a straight leg lead.

17. The speed of lead leg lift determines leg speed of hurdle clearance. Try to move the lead foot so fast it cannot be seen!

18. Ideally, as the leading leg is lifted quickly for hurdle clearance at take-off, the arm opposite the lead leg is thrust forcefully straight ahead and down to balance the movement of the lead leg. This brings the body weight forward and down for a thrust across the hurdle. The trunk dips forward from the hips. Think of the shoulder as going forward with the "opposite arm" action at take-off. A "double-arm" action is not recommended, as it interferes with normal sprint action. Ideally, the lead arm is directed toward the hurdle rail.

19. The other arm (on the same side as the lead leg) remains bent at the elbow in a normal sprinting position in readiness to come forward for the first getaway stride after clearance.

20. The head continues facing forward as in normal sprinting alignment.

HURDLE CLEARANCE:

21. The action of the lead leg should be so fast it produces a wide split between the legs after take-off. Then, the trail leg (take-off leg) will come through late but fast as it crosses the hurdle.

22. After full extension of the take-off leg, the heel of the take-off foot is brought immediately to the buttock. Thus the lower leg is folded to the upper leg, permitting the entire trail leg to subsequently clear the hurdle as one unit.

23. The forward lean or body-dip which began on the ground at take-off continues in the air so as to produce a hurdle clearance as flat as possible. As the body crosses the hurdle, the chin should be over or ahead of the knee of the lead leg.

24. The body's center of gravity reaches its zenith before the hurdle and the foot of the lead leg reaches its highest point some 6 to 12 inches (15 to 30 centimeters) in front of the hurdle rail. From the high point, the hurdler comes down across the hurdle in his clearance.

25. Before the seat reaches the hurdle, the lead leg cuts over the hurdle rail and down toward the other side. This lead leg is still straightening as it crosses the rail.

26. When over the hurdle the body-dip places the chest well forward over the thigh (upper leg) of the lead leg. The shoulders remain square to the front. The "opposite arm" remains thrust forward and down, parallel to the lead leg. The arm on the same side as the lead leg is brought back level with the hip, with elbow bent, so that this elbow is roughly over the corresponding hip. The palm of this arm is open and its forearm is pointed forward. It is a good rule to keep the elbows outside the wrists in hurdling. This body-dip results in the center of gravity being lifted only slightly above its rise in normal sprinting. Throughout hurdle clearances in the 120 yards (110m) hurdles race, the head remains at approximately the same level.

27. Ideally, the head should face straight forward at all times, even though some of the best hurdlers such as Martin Lauer (Germany) and Jack Davis (U.S.A.) have dropped their head during the lay-out position over the hurdle.

28. The heel of the lead foot leads as the body drives across the hurdle. The leading foot is aimed at the rail, but is lifted so fast it passes over the bar.

29. The trail leg should start to come through as the lead leg goes down across the hurdle. The crotch should be over the hurdle rail before the trailing knee reaches the bar.

30. As the take-off foot leaves the ground, its heel rises to the buttock, and the knee swings well out to the side and forward to clear the rail.

31. When the trail leg crosses the hurdle rail it is parallel to the ground.

32. The trail leg makes a right angle with the lead leg as it crosses the bar parallel to the ground.

33. When the bulk of the body weight is beyond the hurdle and the lead leg is well on its way to the ground, the trail leg passes over the hurdle rail.

34. As the trail leg crosses the hurdle rail, the foot is "cocked" upward to avoid striking the hurdle with the toes.

35. As the trail leg crosses the rail it is lifted up high at the knee toward and almost to the chest so as to insure an optimum getaway stride of about five (1.52 meters) feet.

36. The foot of the lead leg grounds 3'9" to 4'6" (114 to 137 centimeters) beyond the hurdle after clearance. This landing of the lead leg must be beneath and slightly behind the center of gravity to insure immediate return to sprinting action after hurdle clearance. The extreme body lean over the hurdle decreases to the body angle of normal sprint action as the lead leg grounds to come "off the hurdle" sprinting.

37. As the body pivots over the hurdle in the above described clearance action, thus changing the position of the legs, the arms also change position. The leading arm (opposite arm) swings back, somewhat bent at the elbow, with the hand carried low. It sweeps backward, outside the knee of the trailing leg, which is now moving foward. If the elbow is bent and the hand carried low, a wide novice "swimming" action of this arm may be

avoided. The lower the trunk position in crossing the hurdle, the less vigorous will be the backward swing in this leading (opposite) arm. The other arm (on the same side as the lead leg) now swings forward in coordination with the forward movement of the rear (trail) leg on the opposite side.

38. In the pivoting action across the hurdle, there must be no "posed" position. The legs must move continuously throughout the hurdle clearance.

39. It is sometimes claimed that the lead leg is snapped down as hurdle clearance is made. Actually the lead leg moves down in reaction to the upward lifting of the trail leg. Attempting to snap the lead leg down would cause the trunk to rise upright as a result of reaction. If the lead leg is snapped down and the trunk comes prematurely upright, this loss of lean may cause the trail leg to drop, possibly resulting in the foot striking the rail as it is brought through. Rather than attempting to snap the lead leg down, lift the trail leg through high and attempt to run away from the hurdle. The faster the trail leg is pulled through, the faster the lead leg will move to the ground. This is not to suggest the trail leg should be "hurried" (causing a jump over the hurdle), nor that it should be delayed. A fast moving bent lead leg at take-off will ensure a proper split between thighs and the correct position of the trail leg as it is pulled through to assist the grounding of the lead leg.

40. Hitting the hurdle with the ankle of the trail leg is usually due to insufficient body-dip over the hurdle.

41. An insufficient or short first getaway stride is caused by lack of trail leg lift.

42. The length of the first getaway stride is often the key to proper stride length between hurdles. This first stride after clearance must be a hard driving effort of about five feet (150 centimeters). Examination of spike marks left on the track may assist in detecting faults in this regard.

43. In correct hurdle clearance, the lead foot lands beyond the hurdle almost directly in line with the point of take-off, although the lead leg may cut slightly across the path of the body's center of gravity.

44. The recovery of the trail leg's sweeping action across the hurdle may result in the first getaway stride being slightly out of alignment with the other strides. If the lead and trail feet land significantly askew from directly in line with the take-off point, this may be remedied in training by sprinting over hurdles placed across a lane line, and ensuring that each foot lands on this line a proper distance from the hurdle after clearance.

45. After a hurdle is cleared the eyes should focus on the next hurdle rail rather than on the ground.

46. The major preoccupation in hurdle training should be with fast hurdling. Too much sprinting with sprinters may cause the hurdler to change the pattern of strides to the first hurdle.

47. Sprint the final 15 yards (14 meters) to the finish. Any dip, finish action used must come in the last one or two strides. 110m is 10¾" or 27cm longer than 120 yards.

48. Hurdling should be considered a sprint race over obstacles, and the action throughout should involve as little interruption as possible in sprinting form. Although for purposes of description and analysis it may be convenient to separate hurdle clearance into various phases, it is in reality a continuous coordinated effort, and not a series of separate parts.

49. Think of hurdling as making room for the obstacles during the sprint race by changing the position of the limbs in relation to the center of gravity while raising it as little as necessary for clearance.